The Official Guide to Wine Snobbery

The Official Guide to Wine Snobbery

Leonard S. Bernstein

ELM TREE BOOKS

London

to Jerry

First published in Great Britain 1983
by Elm Tree Books (Hamish Hamilton Ltd
Garden House 57–59 Long Acre London WC2E 9JZ

Portions of this book have been previously published
in slightly different form in *House Beautiful*, *The
New York Times*, and *Signature* magazine

Illustrations and book design by Terry M. Fehr

British Library Cataloguing in Publication Data

Bernstein, Leonard S.
 The official guide to wine snobbery.
 1. Wine and wine making
 I. Title
 641.2′2   TP548
 ISBN 0–241–11076–9

Printed in Great Britain by
Redwood Burn Ltd, Trowbridge, Wiltshire

Contents

PART II

PART III

Introduction

Reginald, the ultimate wine snob, was walking on Fifth Avenue at six o'clock in the morning when he was struck from behind by a small truck making a wine delivery. As the truck swerved, three bottles cracked, the contents spilling all over the floor. The truck disappeared and Reginald could later supply no details as to the size or model or color.

"Did you see anything at all?" asked the Inspector.

"Nothing," said Reginald.

"Well, were you *aware* of anything, a sound perhaps, or an odor?"

Reginald returned to the moment of the accident—an odor?—why yes, there was an odor. Actually it was a bouquet; it was the bouquet of wine.

"Find a wine delivery truck," said Reginald, "that is carrying some 1966 Château Margaux."

The story is a wine-snob story, outrageous, flamboyant and elegant. If you aspire to wine snobbery you must tell the story of Reginald, and somewhere in the far recesses of your consciousness you must believe that it really could happen.

Wine snobbery, of course, is part showmanship, part sophistication, part knowledge and part bluff. Do you really want to be a wine snob?

Well then, you must learn about sniffing and twirling; you must learn about decanting; you must learn about clearing the palate; and you must learn about letting the wine breathe. You must be prepared to argue drink-red-wine-with-meat, and you must be prepared to argue drink-white-wine-with-meat. You must learn the IN wines and the OUT wines, the IN years and the OUT years, and above all the IN things to say; the IN stories. So clearly you need a guide, and this is it: THE OFFICIAL GUIDE TO WINE SNOBBERY.

First, one must recognize that there is a mystique about drinking wine. There is something elite about those people who really know which wine to order with ris de veau—or can fake it. Their friends often hate them, sometimes love them, but always secretly envy them. Wine snobs, sensing that this knowledge (or posture) commands a certain respect, seek to secure their privileged status.

And so certain rituals and courtesies—even affectations—have appeared, and the GUIDE will introduce you to them.

Understand that this is not a treatise about appreciating wine; there are countless books—even, heaven knows, Adult Education courses—for that. This is a guide to Wine Snobbery. This is concerned with impressing people. Follow these suggestions and you will intimidate the sommeliers in the world's finest restaurants. Ignore them, and you will be laughed at in Burger King.

PART I

Letter to the editor in an old English wine journal

There seems to be a thin line
between wine sophistication and wine snobbery.
Can you clarify the distinction?

Elizabeth

Dear Elizabeth:
A wine sophisticate knows that *1970* was a
great year for Château Latour.
A wine snob knows the name of the cellarmaster.

CLEARING THE PALATE

In the world of wine snobbery there is no statement that will admit you into the fraternity more immediately than "clearing the palate." It is the password. Clearing the palate is what one does in order to best determine the quality of the wine. Specifically, one chews on a corner of bread which absorbs the foreign flavors on the tongue and prepares the tasting mechanism for the subtle demands of the wine.

Probably it is the curious phraseology that makes it so snobbish, but also it is the notion that any clearing must be done. After all, nobody talks about clearing the palate to taste anything else. But the wine fraternity is not like anything else and has its own language to describe some of the delicate traditions necessary to the appreciation of the art.

So if you want to be a wine snob, you have to go around clearing your palate all the time; that's all there is to it. Of course it would be possible (and incredibly embarrassing) to clear your palate at the wrong time, or to use the wrong thing to clear it with. I mean, you can't gargle with Listerine. There are only two things to clear your palate with, water and bread. Bread is much more snobbish because it makes it apparent that that's what you are doing. If

you use water, someone could think you are merely thirsty. And since one does not *announce* that one is clearing the palate, it must, nevertheless, be made fairly obvious.

So when the waiter brings the wine and pours some into your glass, don't taste it right away. Reach for a breadstick or a corner of crust and chew it for a moment. The event does not demand fanfare; it just demands doing. The others at the table cannot help but notice, and you will be recognized by one and all as a first-rate snob.

There is a way to do it wrong, and my former friend Vernon managed it. The waiter brought the wine and poured some in his glass. As this was happening Vernon was reaching discreetly for the bread. There was no bread so Vernon commanded the waiter to bring some so he could clear his palate. Vernon has never been permitted to order or taste the wine again.

You see, snobbery is a bit like wearing jewelry. It is entirely possible to wear too much.

THE UNUSUAL BOTTLE

The scene is a pleasant French restaurant. The waiter brings the wine list and someone hands it to you—the acknowledged wine snob. You have your reputation to protect and you consider the list carefully. Finally you tell the waiter, "Number 623, please."

"Which wine did you order?" someone asks.

"A Beaujolais."

"A Beaujolais? How can you order a Beaujolais? We're all having fish."

"A white Beaujolais."

End of conversation—you have done it again. You have, with just the right shade of arrogance and condescension, put everyone in his place and ruined the entire evening for the questioner. How dare he challenge your choice? It would be perfectly O.K. to order a Beaujolais with fish. Not the best choice perhaps, but entirely reasonable and just a bit snobbish also.

But essentially what you have accomplished is finding THE UNUSUAL BOTTLE, a technique the wine snob can hardly be without.

A white Beaujolais is perfect, and it remains perfect whether there are questions or not. The mere serving of a white Beaujolais will impress your friends and associates. And if there are no questions before it is served, there may possibly be a question afterwards. Somebody who is quite sure that Beaujolais is only red might say, "Did you know it was white?"

This is an awkward situation and the wine snob should not relish it. The question is so naïve that the obvious putdown, "Of course," doesn't work. Everyone at the table is immediately embarrassed for the questioner. If you destroy him you appear not snobbish but brutal. The only thing to say is "I might not have known, but it was indicated on the wine list." There are times, you see, when you can't be snobbish—you have to be tolerant. It taxes the wine snob's patience, but it must be done.

There are other bottles almost as good as white Beaujolais. In a crowd that knows a little about wine but not a whole lot, a Chassagne-Montrachet—red, that is—carries the day. Most people associate the Montrachets with white wine, and indeed that is what Montrachet, Puligny-Montrachet and Chassagne-Montrachet are noted for; perhaps the finest dry white wine in the world. A red Chassagne-Montrachet is an UNUSUAL BOTTLE. And it is a good wine, not simply an attempt to be unconventional.

Another extremely snobbish bottle is a white Châteauneuf-du-Pape. Again, the wine is widely known as red; the element of surprise is exquisite. In fairness, after the shock subsides, someone might ask, "If you were going to order a white, couldn't you do better than a Châteauneuf-du-Pape?" And they would be right. But count on the element of surprise and supreme self-confidence to immobilize such challenges. The wine snob scores again.

DECANTING

Nothing in the world of wine permits the snob more showmanship than decanting. And there are two legitimate reasons for it: to expose the wine to air, allowing it to breathe, and to remove the sediment that forms in older red wines.

Consider the nature of the craft. The classic art of decanting calls for holding the bottle carefully on its side and lighting a candle behind the neck and shoulder of the bottle. The flame illuminates the wine as it passes through the neck, and as soon as sediment appears—usually in the last inch or two of wine—the pouring stops and the dregs are discarded. The procedure is ceremonial but not necessarily pretentious. The object, then, is to make it pretentious.

Non-snobs decant the wine before the guests arrive. Dinner at their homes is never any fun. First-class wine snobs wait until about a half hour before dinner, and then quietly but obviously slip away from apéritifs, retire to the dining room, which is hopefully not out of sight of the living room, and begin the pageant. If nobody follows, the wine snob asks someone to come along and help, thus announcing the event. If you are the guest at a wine snob's home, and this event is announced (however

discreetly), you are expected in the dining room at once—nor would a few well-timed ohs and ahs be out of order.

If you return home envious, anxious to perform the decanter soliloquy at *your* next dinner party, remember this: Decant a wine that needs decanting. That means a wine that has sediment, because the candlelight ceremony is obviously not needed for decanting a wine only to allow it to breathe. You need a wine that is at least ten years old, and you have to hold it to the light to see if sediment has collected. If you decant a wine that does not need it—a five-year-old red Bordeaux for example—you will find yourself the leading character in one of those wine stories that get around town in less than three weeks.

Well then, how to be sure? How to purchase a wine that has sediment? You can't after all bring a flashlight into the wine shop, nor can you hold each bottle up to the light. You *could* buy a vintage Port. Be certain the label reads "vintage Port" and not "of the vintage." A vintage Port must be bottled two years after the vintage, and anything older than ten years is your best bet to have sediment. A vintage Port, however, can only be served after dinner, but that will allow you to do your act when you have everyone trapped in the dining room. It is a bit gauche, but being a wine snob is not easy; you have to take risks.

THE MYSTERY OF CHATEAU LAFITE

In the life of every wine connoisseur there exists a case of Lafite-Rothschild. It is his medal of honor, his initiation fee into the society, the ultimate statement of distinction. The art connoisseur might own a Degas; the collector of rare musical instruments a Stradivarius. But for the wine connoisseur there is above all Château Lafite.

But just as there are Degas and Degas, a Lafite '66 is not the same as a Lafite '61. Hardly anything is the same as a Lafite '61, and so, very early in my wine career, a case found its way into my life.

I don't deny that I purchased it so I could go around talking about "my case of '61 Lafite," but I bought it during the mid-1960s before it was apparent that the case would have 21-carat snob appeal. It cost me five pounds a bottle. The last I heard it was selling for £125.

One hundred and twenty-five pounds a bottle. That's £14 a glass or about £1.20 a sip. It's also £1.99 a gulp if I'm addressing myself to anyone who would gulp a glass of 1961 Château Lafite-Rothschild.

It would advance my somewhat shaky reputation as a wine connoisseur to suggest that I bought it without hesitation, laid it down in my cellar and forgot about it. But the truth is that I bought it with trepidation, didn't have a cellar to store it, and worried about it ever after. At £125 a bottle, reduced to cubic inch cost, it became the most expensive thing I owned. I couldn't consider drinking it. I was afraid to store it. I was embarrassed to insure it, and too stingy to serve it. The only thing I seemed able to do was worry about it.

The whole thing was out of proportion. This was, after all, a bottle of wine. Wine—to be opened with dinner, swirled around the glass, sniffed, tasted, enjoyed and then forgotten about. Alas, my wife says there is no dinner she can ever cook that will measure up to one hundred and twenty-five pounds' worth of wine.

I knew very early that the case was ill fated. I purchased it only to enhance my credentials, and like the art collector who buys a few careless lines by Picasso so he can talk about *his Picasso*, I was soon to reap the rewards of excessive pride.

I left the case in the cellar of the wine merchant, who told me that he would hold it until it "was ready." That was an important consideration because wine does not store well in my basement. I sort of forgot about it after that, although I was remotely conscious that the 1961 Bordeaux were developing very well and climbing in price. However, the matter held no immediacy. The wine was stored and safe. Some day, I thought, in about five years I'll think about what I want to do with it.

During the year 1968 I received a notice from the wine merchant, requesting shipping instructions for the case. This was a serious matter because I couldn't store it, and I couldn't ship such a treasure to a warehouse.

Then I remembered that he had promised to hold it until it was ready, and everybody knew that '61 Lafite was not ready in 1968. Still, I knew it would be an argument. I had not purchased anything recently in his shop, and it was clear that he wanted to get the case out of his basement. A confrontation already. And not a sip of wine had I enjoyed.

"You promised, when I bought it, that you would hold it until it was ready. Are you saying that the 1961 Lafite is ready?"

"The 1961 Lafite may not be ready in our lifetime," he said. "I have to ship it sometime or other."

Damn it, I thought, he's probably right about that.

"Well, how about holding it a little longer?"

"Another year or two—that's it," he said. And that was that.

Two years flew by and I got another notice. Sweat broke out when I saw the envelope. The wine had doubled in price in two years. I still had nowhere to store it.

"It's still not ready!" I shouted on the phone.

"Who are you talking to?" asked the voice politely.

"I want Mr. Fleming. He said he wouldn't make me take my case of '61 Lafite until it was ready. It's still not ready."

"Mr. Fleming is no longer with us," he said.

I had exhausted the possibilities at the wine merchant and I needed a new approach. I lay awake nights thinking about it—wondering where to put it. Finally, there was only one choice.

My local wine shop on Long Island had a cellar, of course, and I had been buying a fair amount of wine there. I asked the proprietor if he would hold a case of 1961 Lafite.

"Sixty-one Lafite?" he asked. "Do you know how much that's worth?"

"I know," I said, embarrassed. Here I buy my £1.99 Vouvray and Beaujolais from him, and he's thinking I buy my Lafite from a fancy shop in the city.

"I got it as a gift," I lied.

So the case went down in his basement, and I had anxiety attacks thinking about his stockboys ripping off a bottle. Meanwhile I hadn't had a taste.

Things went along quietly for a few years, as the wine escalated to £125 a bottle, and then one day the wine shop was sold. No problem, I figured; I'll just go in and introduce myself to the new owner. He'll get my business, so he should be willing to hold the treasure-case in storage.

And it was no problem until a year later—1975, I

believe—when I drove past the shop one day and saw the huge lock on the door and the sign in the window: The shop was in bankruptcy, and all the wine was to be sold at auction.

My mouth turned chalk-dry, and I stood there immobilized. I finally bolted into the hardware store next door, where the owner said that the wine shop proprietor had gotten into financial difficulty and had simply left town. No one knew where he was. The assets of the shop had been seized by the receiver to satisfy the debts.

SEIZED! My case of '61 Lafite—having suffered all other adventures except being tasted—was now seized.

I called the receiver's office. They were most polite and helpful. They asked me to appear with evidence that I had such a case in storage at the shop and they would release it. Evidence? How was I to produce evidence? My only evidence was the proprietor.

I took two Valiums and called my lawyer. He pointed to a depressing lack of proof. I told him if I had proof I wouldn't need him.

"No need to get angry," he said. And then he outlined his plan of legal action. I know something about lawyers' plans of action—they are always expensive. It sounded like about two hundred and fifty pounds' worth to me.

"We have to get a restraining order," he said.

I could see it all unfolding—a battle through the courts—appeal after appeal. The next three years in and out of courtrooms. For that much money and aggravation I could bid on the case myself and buy it back at the auction. The ultimate humiliation.

I had no idea what to do, but that night I received a phone call.

"My name is Joe DeAngelis," he said. "I have your case of Lafite."

RANSOM, I thought.

"How much do you want, DeAngelis?" I asked, using my gravel voice.

"No," he said. "You have it wrong. I'm one of the stockboys. I knew you had the Lafite in storage, and I knew they would auction it off with the rest of the cases. So I snuck it out of the shop and took it home."

FRAUD, I thought.

Here's what happens, I thought: We make a time and place to exchange the case. Probably somewhere secret like the back alley of Newsome's Bike Shop. I tell him I'll be wearing red. He says he walks with a slight limp. We meet. I take the case. The sirens sound. We're surrounded. Handcuffs. Anything I say will be used against me. A federal crime: dealing in stolen goods.

"Give me your number, DeAngelis, I'll call you back." And I rushed out to a phonebox.

"Listen, Mr. Bernstein," said DeAngelis, sensing my poise and calm, "there's nothing wrong. I know it's your case. It's been there a few years. Why should you lose it? If you want I'll drive it over to your house tonight."

I looked around outside the phone booth. There was a guy walking across the street in a trench coat. He came a little closer. It was my neighbor, Stanley.

"O.K., DeAngelis, bring it over. And thanks."

Some stories end with bloodshed and intrigue, but DeAngelis turned out, simply, to be a nice young man who had recognized an injustice and thought he would do something about it. I forced ten dollars on him which he really wanted no part of and which I still feel guilty about. The case went down to my basement.

There it rests as the furnace goes on and off and as my son and his friends play Ping-Pong nearby. I go down to look at it, worried that it is all right—worried that it is turning bad—worried that the oil-burner man will lift a few bottles. It is, still, a £125 bottle of wine.

It has cost me grey hairs and sleepless nights, tension and anxiety. But this I have learned: There are men who are born to Lafite-Rothschild and men who are born to Beaujolais, and I know which one I am.

LETTING
THE WINE
BREATHE

There is much controversy among wine snobs about whether a red wine needs to be opened in advance of serving so the wine can be exposed to air. We will avoid the merits of each position since we are not interested in being right, but only in being snobbish. There is considerable snobbery in each position, and the best route to instant recognition is to contradict whatever the waiter does.

You order a 1971 red Burgundy, and the captain brings the bottle but does not uncork it. You tell him, "I think you ought to let it breathe a bit."

You order the same wine, and the waiter uncorks it and says, "I think it ought to breathe awhile. I'll serve it in a few minutes." You answer politely (but with an edge of condescension), "Why don't you pour it now; it will open up in the glass."

Opening up is what a red wine does when it is exposed to air. It softens and mellows. Which is why most wine snobs let a better red wine breathe. It's not a bad phrase to use, being regarded by true snobs as a legitimate part of the vocabulary.

ADJECTIVES

The ultimate wine snob, Richard Pratt, is found in Roald Dahl's story "Taste." Pratt had the "curious, rather droll habit of referring to wine as though it were a living being."

"A prudent wine," he would say, "rather diffident and evasive, but quite prudent." Or, "a good-humored wine, benevolent and cheerful—slightly obscene, perhaps, but nonetheless good-humored."

The reader might think this quaint and charming—an interesting aberration for one of Mr. Dahl's perverse characters, but Roald Dahl has more credibility. He knows about wine and he knows about wine snobs, and he is not about to invent the dialogue. What Roald Dahl says about Richard Pratt is heard all around town where wine snobs hang out. So we can't pass over this casually; if we worship wine snobbery we had better pray at the right altar.

It is true, alas, that wine is described with human adjectives, so the snob need only consider which adjectives are acceptable. It would be possible, for example, to describe a wine as assertive, but impossible to describe it as athletic. A wine might be diffident or shy, but it could hardly be described as awkward. It is a fine line, and it is crossed when you impart a physical characteristic to the wine. An emotional or psychological characteristic is perfect; a physical characteristic usually doesn't work.

There is no primer on this subject; the emerging wine snob must develop his own repertoire. Richard Pratt might have found a wine diffident; you might find it charming. There is no right and wrong—there is only the poetry of the description.

Well, perhaps there is some right and wrong, because Dahl's story happens in London, and what passes for snobbery in London might be plain stupidity in New York. And in fact, if Richard Pratt recited his observations even in the most venerated New York wine societies, I suspect there would be some consternation at his table at the very least.

So even emotional and psychological characteristics require some thought. Yes, a wine might be described as charming—a fairly general adjective. No, it cannot be described as diffident—the quality is too precious, too effete.

Yes, a wine might be described as cheerful—it's probably the perfect word for a Beaujolais. No, it cannot be described as benevolent; that is too complex, too subtle, *too* human.

The wine snob reads Hugh Johnson and André Simon and gets a feeling for the right words. Snobbery demands imagination, even daring, but above all it demands taste and discernment.

RED
WINE WITH
MEAT

There are wine snobs who argue, "Drink red wine with meat," and there are wine snobs who argue, "Drink white wine with meat," and both of these wine snobs must be you.

This has always been the classic area of wine snobbery. You order a red wine with veal francese, and someone at the table collapses in a fit of despair. The following week you order a white wine with the same entrée and you are met with the same chorus of disapproval. Both wine snobs can't be right, but both have succeeded in intimidating you. What to do?

Remember this: Nothing is *right*. There are no hard-and-fast rules about which wine to order with which food, so you are as entitled to act like a snob as they are. Of course they may have been practicing longer, but the foundation stone on which you thought their expertise rested does not exist. Your preference is as good as their preference, your arrogance as good as their arrogance. The key is to be assertive. Don't ask everyone what they would like. Just say, "I think we might enjoy a red Bordeaux with veal tonight." Close the wine list and place the order.

I suppose a minor word of caution is called for.

There are no absolute rules about red-wine-with-meat, but there are guidelines. Wine does complement food, and a good marriage of wine and food will make both more enjoyable. There are strong wines like good Bordeaux and Burgundy, Italian Barolo, Chianti Riservas, and better German Rhines. There are also strong dishes like cassoulet or beef bourguignon. Marry the wine to the dish; that's all there is to it.

Conversely, there are lighter wines—Beaujolais, Bardolino, Chablis and Moselle—and they are happier with lighter dishes. Use your judgment as to which entrées are light and which are heavy. You know as well as anyone else.

THE SNUBBING OF LE PAVILLON

At the age of twenty-three I knew I was destined to a life of wine snobbery. It happened quite by accident; I was two years out of college and on a very tight budget. Still, it was our anniversary, and dinner in New York seemed appropriate. A quiet French restaurant, perhaps. Something for around five dollars a person. It was possible then.

I mentioned it to a business acquaintance. Something special, I said. I doubt that I mentioned the five-dollar part.

"Try Le Pavillon," he said. "It's quite nice."

Le Pavillon. I had never heard of it, but it had the right melody.

I called. Reservations for Leonard Bernstein. I didn't have enough sense in those days to realize that one does not make reservations in the name of Leonard Bernstein whether it is your name or not.

Anyway, I did. And when we arrived it was apparent that they were expecting someone else because there was a reception line at the door. But it was me and not HIM, and we were seated accordingly.

But that's not the story. The story is how I got even with Le Pavillon.

Dinner, I will tell you, was less than delightful.

We were confused by the menu; we were startled by the prices. I knew at once that I didn't have the money for the most limited culinary excursion. "Do you have some money?" I whispered to Rita. "You do? Well, pass it to me under the table."

We were intimidated further by the sommelier. (I didn't know then that's what he was.) He was just another guy in a fancy outfit, with a chain around his neck. He assumed we would have wine, and simply asked which one we preferred. "Whatever you suggest," I mumbled.

I can still see him standing there, pouring some wine in my glass, and waiting, waiting at attention, and then shifting from one foot to the other.

"Would you care to taste it?" he asked, finally.

I suppose, somewhere inside of me, I knew right then that he was the enemy.

We stumbled through dinner, dreadfully self-conscious, using the wrong fork for salad, using the wrong knife for butter, pouring the wine myself as the sommelier came charging down the aisle offended and indignant.

Happily, the check arrived. I undertipped the waiter, forgot the head waiter, forgot the sommelier—headed toward the door almost at a run and found myself, finally, in the open air of Park Avenue and Fifty-seventh Street.

And there, slowly—the enemy behind me—I began to smolder. Smoke turned to fire, and I vowed—as only the young can vow—that I would get even. Get even with a restaurant. Imagine.

I knew immediately, there on Fifty-seventh Street, what I had to do first: I had to learn about wine. I had to prepare for the next encounter with the sommelier. And if I had little sense, I had lots of energy. I read and I studied. I joined wine-tasting groups and I crashed every event that would allow me to try both the elegant and the mediocre wines of the world.

Time went by. I tried some good restaurants; I grew less awkward. Le Pavillon still loomed as the Matterhorn, but I knew it was only a question of time.

And seven years later—trained, tempered, and lean as a fighter before the main event—I knew I was ready.

We arrived. I remember the details precisely. We were seated. The lavender jacket took the order; the green jackets would serve dinner. The black jacket was the sommelier. He wore his chain, the tastevin; he was seven years older.

We ordered cocktails, and they were served in huge Burgundy glasses. As we sipped, considering the menu, the sommelier asked which wine we would like with dinner.

"I'd like to see the list," I said. The moment had arrived.

Now it has to be said, I knew every bottle on the wine list. I knew the year and the grower and the grape, and a whole lot more than any sensible person ought to know. I also knew which were the sophisticated bottles; those bottles that might have been outstanding in a mediocre year, or those bottles that were underpriced in an outstanding year. In short, I knew which bottles would impress the hell out of the sommelier, and I was damn well going to order one of them.

Would it be a Cos D'Estournel '55? No, overpriced. A Bonnes Mares '58? Maybe. The year was underrated, the price was reasonable, the vintner was first-rate. I traveled through the list, and finally came to a Pétrus '52, at least seven or eight dollars less expensive than it should have been. The '52s were first starting to open up. It had been a curious year, the wines heavy with tannin and developing slowly, the Pétrus probably a few years more mature than its counterparts in Bordeaux. It was perfect.

"The '52 Pétrus," I said, rather matter-of-fact.

He was stunned. I knew it. He had judged me for a Beaujolais.

It was so delicious—seven years' delicious—let me repeat it.

"The '52 Pétrus," I said.

I handed him the list, and at that moment the most extraordinary thing began to happen: My head started to swim from the cocktail. Impossible, I thought. I could drink three cocktails with dinner if I wasn't having wine. And then I recalled the day: a business day, exceptionally tense and no time for lunch. Total food consumed: one glass of orange juice; two cups of coffee.

The alcohol had entered a starved bloodstream, and was now ricocheting around between my brain and my stomach.

They brought the appetizer. I didn't want it, but I thought I had better have it. Besides, I had paid for it. Remember, it was me against Le Pavillon.

My head was spinning, and slowly the inevitable nausea began. It was going to be close whether it would take over. I drank some water, tasted a corner of crust, fought desperately. It would be sad to lose the battle, but a tragedy to lose on a technicality.

Of course I had forgotten the Pétrus, and just as I sat there, on the fence, maybe to topple, maybe to recover—seventeen guys in different-colored jackets kaleidoscoped before me, the sommelier holding the basket containing the treasure.

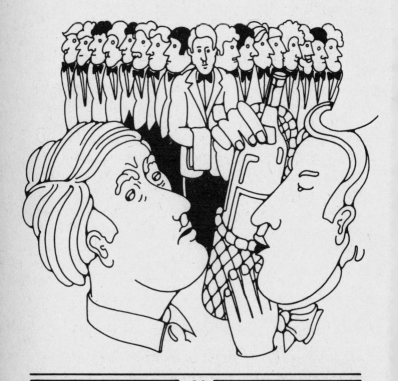

"Shall I open it and let it breathe?" he asked.

The mere sight of it caused me to sway. There was no possibility of having even one glass of wine. I would have settled then just to make it through dinner.

But there he stood, the sommelier, my enemy: reserved, respectful, repentant.

If he poured the wine and I didn't drink it, I would lose. If he poured the wine and I did drink it, they would have to call the doctor; I would still lose. If they didn't pour the wine after all that ceremony—if I sent it back unopened—I would lose worst of all.

It wasn't my head that decided but my digestive system. "Take it back," I muttered.

"Take it back?" He was incredulous. The gold jackets looked at the lavender jackets. Everyone shook his head.

I waved my hand, negatively. Anything to get him out of there. "I've changed my mind," I said. I couldn't think of anything else to say.

He glared at me and cleared his throat, realizing at once that I was a Beaujolais type after all. Nor did he ever again darken the area around my table.

It was a first-round knockout. Seven years of training and I didn't make it to round two. It was the ultimate humiliation.

Someone said later that I had won after all. That to send back a bottle of '52 Pétrus at Le Pavillon was the ultimate victory. That sounds good, and I'd like to believe it, but it simply comes apart.

The truth is that one does not get even with Le Pavillon, and before another seven years passed, Le Pavillon closed without giving me a return bout. As I wander now by Park Avenue and Fifty-seventh Street, I affect my battle stance, challenging the enemy to come out fighting. But the walls are silent, and even I know it is the shouting of the fool.

THE CORRECT WINE WORDS: BOUQUET, TASTE AND COLOR

Wine has its own vocabulary, and this is invaluable to the wine snob. Just as tennis fanatics talk of topspin lobs and compare Adidas to Nike, so must the wine snob cultivate his own exclusivity.

BOUQUET

While you might *smell* a rose or describe the *scent* of fine perfume, you don't do either with a glass of wine. Wine has neither smell nor scent nor odor; wine has bouquet. In extremely snobbish surroundings wine has a nose, although that is really the language of the inner chamber.

The experienced wine snob, having carried on awhile about the bouquet, proceeds to announce certain characteristics. It is urgently important to learn which characteristics are acceptable and which are not. For instance, if you think a wine's bouquet resembles—what shall we say?—Chanel #5, you are best off keeping your opinion to yourself. Wines, generally, are thought to resemble the aromas of flowers, herbs, spices and wood, the best of all of these being violets. You are sure to be regarded as a first-class wine snob if you discern the aroma of violets in a red wine. If you don't, black currants, cedar and vanilla are acceptable, in that order. Naturally you make much of this, exhibiting considerable excitement and, of course, conviction. Conviction above all else; after all, who can contradict you? The best they can say is that they *do not* detect the aroma of violets, at which time it will be apparent that their experience is limited and they will feel appropriately humiliated.

TASTE

It's hard to describe the taste of wine and harder yet if you want to be snobbish about it. A good rule might be: If the descriptive word can be used for food it cannot be used for wine. You might refer to roast beef as delicious, and that should signal you to stay away from "delicious" when the wine is served.

One of the terrific wine words is "big." That comes as a bit of a surprise since "big" is a rather inelegant word. Still, it has captured the wine drinker's fancy, and whenever a strong red wine is served you can automatically describe it as big and be certain to hold your own at the table. White wines may also be described as big, but you can get into trouble here because the judgment is more subtle and requires more training.

If someone steals "big" when you are looking at the menu, you can retreat to "body." The words are almost interchangeable. You thus join the other wine snob at the table, and although you now have a partner, the both of you can lord it over the others.

"Finesse" is another perfect word for wine. First of all it is hard to contradict. Second, it sounds elegant. "Finesse" is used to describe wine that has balance and subtlety and harmony. It can be used for red or white wines, and it is a most impressive term.

There are, of course, words to avoid. You will occasionally hear wine snobs use "breed" and "race" to describe a wine that has finesse and character. These are insecure wine snobs, reaching into the clouds to be sophisticated. Remember that although the wine snob may have his nose in the sky, his two feet should stay on the ground.

COLOR

Of course color is an important characteristic of wine, and at any table grave discussions will be held over color. It is consequently important for the neophyte to learn some of the good color words and the bad color words.

Generally a good red wine will have a deep ruby color, and it is quite all right to comment accordingly. The absolutely most snobbish way of judging the color is to hold the wine glass against the white tablecloth, providing a background for judging the depth of the red. Another way, although entirely second-rate, is to hold it up to the light. At any wine tasting you can separate the lords from the commoners by observing who holds his glass at the table edge and who holds it up to the chandelier.

So you can describe a red wine's color as deep or ruby, and you can describe a white wine's color as you see it—straw, or amber, or pale-with-a-touch-of-green. The latter is a characteristic of Chablis and Pouilly-Fumé, and the description will win you a round of applause at any gathering.

It is also possible to go too far in describing color. An emerging wine snob once read an article in a British journal that described a Burgundy as having a deep robe. He brought this back from London and sprang it on the first wine tasting he attended. The table stood painfully silent and the young man has been forced to move to Cincinnati. Never say robe on this side of the Atlantic. Whether or not you say it in England I do not know and do not care. It is hard enough to keep up with snobbery in America.

COMPLEXITY, BALANCE AND FINISH

Bouquet, taste and color are perfectly good wine words—until you run into Reginald. In Reginald's company the character of the language changes, and while observations related to taste and color are not inappropriate, neither are they likely to engage Reginald's attention for more than a fleeting moment.

Accordingly, the wine snob in training is properly advised to consider more subtle distinctions such as balance and complexity. Don't be unnerved by this; nobody knows what complexity means. Not even Reginald knows what complexity means, and Reginald knows everything.

A tenacious attachment to scholarship is not necessarily a prerequisite of wine snobbery. That is the value of a word like "complexity"; it lives in the twilight zone of wine language. If you risk a statement about the rainfall levels in Chablis during 1975, it's bound to be challenged by some wine-neurotic who was over there measuring it. With complexity, you can go on forever.

Which is why, in the stratospheric regions of wine snobbery, everyone uses words like complexity, balance and finish. They are words that permit ambiguity to resemble erudition. Nevertheless, this is the language, so you might as well learn it.

COMPLEXITY

To the extent that anyone understands this word it means that the structure of the wine is not simple. ("Structure": not a bad word to use if Reginald is nearby.) The wine is not easy to taste and appreciate; it demands that the taster contribute some background and understanding. A complex wine is like a complex symphony. Tchaikovsky might be easy to appreciate on first hearing; Mozart requires a little more exposure and concentration. As there are complexities in melody, there are complexities in wine.

Now that we've cleared that one up. . . .

BALANCE

An important word, "balance" means that all the components of the wine—the fruit, the acid, the tannin, the sugar—are in a state of harmony. Fortunately, what constitutes "a state of harmony" is subject to no universal law, and therefore one may observe that a wine is unbalanced without

written confirmation from the Bordeaux Chamber of Commerce.

Wine sometimes tastes acidic, sometimes tastes thin, and that may indicate that the wine is out of balance. Even if it doesn't, a comment to that effect in Reginald's crowd will earn you a good deal of respect.

FINISH

This is a lovely word that wine snobs have adopted to describe aftertaste, and who can blame them? "Aftertaste" is an inelegant word, best used for describing medicine. Actually the phenomenon is the same: "Finish" simply means the taste sensation that remains in the mouth as the wine is swallowed.

If the taste disappears you will hear it said that the wine finishes "short." If the taste remains, sort of filling up your mouth, it will be said that the wine has a "long" or "lingering" finish.

It is generally true that the better the wine, the longer the finish, so here's another word that can be tossed around. The emerging wine snob should consider, however, that while it's safe to mention that almost any Bonnes Mares or Musigny has a long finish, it doesn't follow that you can announce that a Beaujolais has a short finish. A Beaujolais is supposed to have a short finish.

Complexity, balance and finish: You will hear them in the best circles. More important, you will never hear them challenged; they are too elusive, too personal, too introspective. Add them promptly to your wine vocabulary and use them without hesitation in the company of anyone who looks like his name might be Reginald.

THE FIVE "IN" WINES OF THE WORLD — and some that aren't

Last week, at a very sophisticated cocktail party, I bumped into Reginald once again. In 1962 Reginald laid down ten cases of 1959 Château Latour, paying four pounds a bottle and watching it rise to £125. Consequently, he cuts a dramatic presence at the cocktail parties around town although certain hostesses admit their real hope is that he might bring along a bottle or two.

Since Reginald is the high priest of wine snobbery, aspiring snobs consult with Reginald to find out what is currently IN and OUT. Don't think just because Beaujolais was IN last year that it is IN this year, anymore than hemlines stay the same from one fashion season to the next.

Of course I'm not in Reginald's class—nobody is in Reginald's class—and so I take advantage of every opportunity to stay in touch with the changing styles.

"It used to be," said Reginald, "that Bordeaux was IN and California was OUT, and you could pretty well judge a person's character by that standard. But lately the French wines, riding the crest of IN-ness, have approached tidal wave prices." (Reginald has a colorful way of speaking.) "At the same time, rumors started circulating about questionable origins. Word had it that a lot of wine was shipped out of Algeria, and yet not a lot of bottles with Algerian labels. A scandal, certainly, and IN-ness does not stand up well under scandal."

I was hoping for a quick answer—just enough to make an impression—but Reginald does not give true or false answers to wine questions.

"While the French wines were suffering," he continued, "the California wineries were growing up. Blind tastings were being won by David Bruce and Freemark Abbey against the best white Burgundies. It was becoming impossible to ignore the California wine clique."

"This is all fascinating, Reginald, but maybe you could just give me a list of what's IN and what's OUT, and then I would know immediately which people to be impressed by and which people to ignore."

Reginald appeared a bit irritated, but he did admit that there was still a standard, although there were no more absolutes. California wines were no longer in or out. French wines are no longer in or out. What evolved was this: IN-ness had become selective.

Urged to continue, Reginald conceded that secret tastings at The Wine and Food Society, the Chaîne des Rôtisseurs, and The Palm restaurant had produced the following list of what is IN and OUT in wines. A somewhat less-than-precise dedication to Reginald's list could be the end of anyone's social status between New York and Kansas City.

These—says Reginald—are IN:

1. *Château Lafite-Rothschild.* Lafite is IN, has always been in, and always will be in. It is a classic, like Wedgwood or Baccarat. It transcends price fluctuations, rumors and changing fashions. It was the best of the French Bordeaux a hundred years ago and may still be the best today.

Don't make the mistake of thinking that Lafite, at its incredible prices, is out. Don't make the mistake of thinking that anything so luxurious as £125 for a bottle of wine can't be in. Lafite is to wine as Lutèce is to food or Rolls-Royce is to motor cars. It is exquisitely IN.

2. *David Bruce* is marvelously IN as are many of the small California wineries like Freemark Abbey and Trefethen. These houses have, during the past five years, produced wine that has stood up to the great French vineyards. One doesn't have to be chauvinistic to delight in the results of a blind tasting that is won by a David Bruce over a Chassagne-Montrachet or a Corton-Charlemagne. A triumph of the little guy; a gentle slap at the arrogance and hierarchy of Bordeaux and Burgundy. David and Goliath—the world's best-loved story—and yes, a sure sign of IN-ness.

3. *Beaujolais* rides the roller coaster of IN- and OUT-ness, and is presently in. It hasn't the pedigree to remain in—to hold on like Lafite-Rothschild. It is more a wine of intermittent fashion. That is not to say it cannot be excellent wine, but only to say that it cannot be classic.

Today it has become fashionable to see who can drink the first bottle of Beaujolais nouveau, a rather silly race involved with trying to get the wine from grape to glass—from the vines of Burgundy to a restaurant in Paris—in under seven minutes. Much fuss is made of this, although in fact it resembles Grand Prix racing more than serious wine drinking. Nevertheless, the beautiful people are there to taste the new Beaujolais, and who am I to argue with fashion. So Beaujolais is back in, and you can safely regard any opinion to the contrary as boorish and uninformed.

4. *Spanish Rioja* is in. In its quiet way this soft and elegant red wine stands up to the better Bordeaux, and at half the price. You can purchase a vintage Marqués de Riscal for three pounds. Its counterpart in quality from Bordeaux—a Beycheville or a Gruaud-Larose, perhaps—would be five pounds, and no better. Rioja found a foothold in the wine-drinking community about three years ago when the French wine prices soared into outer space. People found the wine smooth and warm, and with a deep subtle flavor. Somehow Rioja attracts only a small group of admirers, one of the fine distinctions of IN-ness.

5. Which would you say is the world's most In white wine? Would it be the magnificent Montrachet, certainly the best of the world's dry white wines, or would it be the German Trocken-beerenauslese? The answer is neither; the winner is *Château d'Yquem*. Yquem is a Sauternes—a dessert wine—that is incredibly rich and sweet without being cloying. It is a curious union of intensity and elegance, probably too good to be served with any food; probably best served after dinner. The proprie-tor of Yquem, the Comte de Lur-Saluces, suggests that it be drunk with foie gras. Someday, in a burst of extravagance, I shall discover whether I agree with him.

These wines are OUT:

1. *Rhines and Moselles,* with the exception of a Trockenbeerenauslese, are out. A Trocken-beerenauslese is in, especially if you can learn to pronounce it.

Rhines and Moselles are out because:

a. They tend toward sweetness when the whole world wants dry wines.

b. The wine labels are intricate, complicated and hard to understand.

c. They have the wrong names. I don't deny that a Geisenheimer Mönchspfad or an Eltviller Lan-genstuck has a certain curious melody, but the merest shade of mispronouncement is so embar-rassing that few wine lovers will risk it.

Other than that, they're in.

2. *Châteauneuf-du-Pape* is out—out—out. It never was in. A good but rather rough wine from the Rhone Valley in France, it has the best name in all of Europe and still can't break the IN circle. Probably the name is too good, a rare combination of poetry and peculiarity that ought to work but doesn't. It is said about this wine—and probably correctly—that people drink it just because of its name. How can anything like that be IN?

3. *Soave Bolla* is an exceptionally popular wine, particularly among people who think it is a wine

name. The wine name is Soave, and a number of houses bottle it, although it is a credit to the Bolla company that they have insinuated their name, like Kleenex, onto the product. Good merchandising, but hardly IN. Soave Bolla is not a bad wine though, especially when the choice is limited to Italian whites, which tend to be somewhat coarse.

4. *Mouton-Cadet*—a blended wine said to be the world's largest-selling red Bordeaux—is the OUT-est. Not only is the wine mediocre, but the advertising is staged to imply that this is a château-bottled wine and indeed has a pedigree like Mouton-Roth-schild, Margaux or Lafite. Well, of course nobody thinks that at two or three pounds a bottle, but the suggestion is there; the inference is there. If imaginative merchandising, aggressive salesmanship and pound volume made a wine IN, Mouton-Cadet would be near the top of the list. As it happens it's near the bottom.

5. I always feel bad that *rosé* is out, and I always secretly hope it will make next year's best-dressed list, sort of in the same way that I hope Woody Allen will make it. Rosé has never pretended to be anything it isn't, a light, unassuming lunch wine—perhaps a picnic wine: no complexity, no delicacy, no elegance. Sadly, one could also say no taste, no character; a flat, uninteresting wine that is hardly ever a best choice even for lunch. It's difficult to be IN under such limiting circumstances and rosé is not IN. To be perfectly candid, there's no sense waiting around for next year's list either.

There you have it; the final word. Reginald's list of what's IN and OUT in wine. Careful attention to the list, plus an occasional bottle of Château d'Yquem, will get you invited to the beautiful-people parties. A slovenly approach will confine you to the late-late show.

VINTAGES

There are baseball snobs who can recite how many doubles Pee Wee Reese hit in 1941 or Enos Slaughter's lifetime batting average, and there are wine snobs who memorize the grafting and pruning techniques in the Napa Valley or the chalk content in the soil of Chablis. Both categories of information transcend what any sensible person ought to know about baseball or wine. Trivia is not an essential characteristic of snobbery, and if you start mentioning pruning techniques—even in the most sophisticated surroundings—you will soon observe a gradual decline in the number of people who care to join you for dinner.

On the other hand, wine snobbery does demand a knowledge of vintages. The vintage of a wine is the year it was pressed—the year the grapes were grown—and a respectable wine snob has a decent recollection of everything from 1950 to the present.

Vintages are a minefield along the road to wine snobbery, the explosion coming when one demonstrates that his accumulation of data exceeds any reasonable purpose.

Well then, what might the aspiring wine snob comment on during the years from 1950 to the present?

1961—it would be dreadful, in any serious group of wine people, to mention that 1961 was a great year. That would be like announcing that Michelangelo painted the Sistine Chapel. It might be O.K. to point out that the '61 Burgundies are not nearly the equal of the '61 Bordeaux. It would also be impressive to mention that Château Palmer—a superb wine but generally not the equal of Lafite or Latour—produced what might be the best 1961 of all.

1952–1953—These two back-to-back vintages gave (and are still giving) wine lovers—especially of

Bordeaux—many happy moments. But they were not simply two great years; each had individual character. The 1952s began as hard wines, heavy in tannin, and they remained hard until perhaps the mid-1960s, many of them into the 1970s. The 1953 vintage was soft from the beginning and the wines were already delightful in the late 1950s. By the late 1970s most of them had started to fade.

1970—A remarkable year. If 1961 was the best of the last thirty years in Bordeaux, 1970 might be second. It's a little early to tell. You are certainly secure in ordering almost any bottle except a wine like Latour or Mouton-Rothschild, which is simply not ready yet.

1950–1958–1967—These were the unheralded years in Bordeaux, the years that produced fine wines that never received the attention they deserved. The year 1950 was immediately over-shadowed by '52 and '53, 1958 by '59 and '61, and 1967 was just one of those peculiar years that did not produce good wine everywhere but did produce it somewhere. On such knowledge is the reputation of a wine snob made.

There may be those who feel that committing thirty years to memory is an excessive price merely to be recognized as a wine snob. Their lethargy is deplorable but there is another way. You can carry around a vintage chart; those charts that rate, on a scale of 1 to 20, every wine in every year. Of course, any old list will not do. You must carry *the* list. *The* list is compiled by Taillevent, which Craig Claiborne called "the best French restaurant in Paris."

One day you will be at a restaurant, and the choice will be between the 1964 and the 1966 red Bordeaux. You can't remember a damned thing about either year and it is clear that your reputation is vanishing on the spot. And so, as Popeye, being humiliated by Pluto, reached for his spinach and became transformed, you pull out your Taillevent vintage chart, pass it along, and say with a slight yawn, "Here, check it out."

Write: Taillevent, 15 rue Lamennais, 75008 Paris, FRANCE.

ETIQUETTE

Almost anybody can drink the wine. The question is: How do you hold the glass? If you answered, "In either hand," they are waiting for you at Clancy's Bar & Grill on Eighth Avenue.

Holding a wine glass is not a two-fisted operation unless you are gulping chilled Chianti out of a jug, an exercise too vulgar to be contemplated in a dissertation on snobbery.

If it's *wine* you are drinking you might want to know that there are four ways to hold the glass.

BY THE BOWL
Holding the bowl between thumb and forefinger is regarded as indecent in any state except New Mexico. True, it's the surest way to steady the wine but it leaves fingerprints on the crystal and it transfers heat between fingers and wine. Nor does it look particularly refined, and certainly refinement is a concern of the wine snob.

BY THE BOWL—*cupped in your hands*
This is the style for sniffing brandy, and it is occasionally acceptable in drinking wine, but only if the wine is served too cold. In such event it demonstrates a discerning palate and an uncom-

promising approach. Red wine is often served too cold, and it is an unmistakable message to the maître d' that you will not have it that way. Of course, if you happen to be invited to a friend's home for dinner, it is also an unmistakable message to the hostess, a point you may wish to consider if your social calendar has unnerving stretches of open space.

BY THE BASE

There are wine enthusiasts with the sleight of hand to hold the base of the wine glass between thumb and forefinger and still control the wine. It's quite a distinguished performance: The thumb rests on top of the base; the forefinger is crooked underneath; and the wine glass appears to float in air. A number of practicing wine snobs have been attempting this for years with less than uniformly successful results. It is the kind of thing—like a half gainer off the high board—that you execute with style or don't bother trying. If you can do it, though, it is immediately recognized as a sure sign of status in the wine community.

BY THE STEM

This is, finally—short of having fingers like Van Cliburn—the best way to hold a wine glass. It combines control with taste and elegance, and keeps your fingers away from the wine. Occasionally, at a tasting, you may observe an extended pinky, and I'm sure I don't have to explain that this is a wine society that you must not feel compelled to immediately join.

So much for holding the glass. Now, what about the glass you are holding? It should be absolutely clear (to judge the color of the wine) and capable of holding at least eight ounces (so that it can be half filled, allowing the bouquet to collect in the upper glass). Baccarat has some nice crystal at about eight pounds a glass and a set of eight will cost you £64. That's not a bargain—I admit it—but a ticket to the theatre of wine snobbery and a tight budget are difficult to reconcile.

ON THE PLAYING FIELDS OF LUTECE

If only I could have said it. It had such class, such distinction. We were at Lutèce, eight wine-and-food fanatics, joined that particular evening by Gael Greene. The air was thick with one-upsmanship.

"Have you tried the '55 Latour?"

"Yes, actually Sam Aaron brought a bottle to a comparative tasting just last week. It was lovely but of course not in the same league with the '45 or the '61. And then there was that bottle of 1929."

We went on this way for an hour or so, trying to establish territory, trying to turn the head of Miss Greene, who would have none of this tomfoolery but who listened politely nevertheless.

I thought I was holding my own, having naturally prepared weeks in advance. One false move in this company and I would be relegated to the jug-wine crowd forever and ever.

About halfway through dinner someone mentioned a small French restaurant which had just opened and was extremely IN. A remarkable coup, and I considered a discreet move toward the washroom for fear that someone would ask if I had been there yet. But I regained my composure and the speaker then mentioned the wine that had been ordered at the new restaurant, and how excellent it was—a very special bottle, something like a '47 Cos d'Estournel. My god, who would order such a bottle? He was running away with the wine snob award.

And then the person next to him said very quietly, "That was my bottle."

We all turned to him at once, not understanding. How could it have been his bottle? It was served in a restaurant.

"When the restaurant opened," he explained, "it had no wine list and it needed one desperately. It couldn't go out in the marketplace and buy wines like '47 Cos d'Estournel—it didn't have the money. Besides, a wine like that could sit in their cellar for years. I know the proprietor well and he was explaining the problem, and so I just told him to use *my* cellar. I live across the street. So his wine list is a compilation of my special bottles, and when someone orders a '47 Cos or a '61 Margaux they send a junior from the kitchen over to my wine cellar, and then repay me for the wines. I leave the key with them. It was the least I could do for a friend starting a new restaurant."

I knew then and I know now that in my entire career as a wine snob I'll never match that.

PART II

At a recent tasting of the wines
of Château Lafite-Rothschild, including
all the great vintages from 1945 to the present,
Eric de Rothschild was asked about
his favorite vintage.

"The '59," he answered, "if you like young wine."

THE CEREMONY OF THE CORK Part I

Do you or do you not pop the cork on a bottle of Champagne? This perplexing problem has divided the wine community, pitting father against son, brother against brother.

The emerging wine snob naturally assumes that you pop the cork—the event promises so much drama, so much flamboyance. He awaits his opportunity, gives the bottle a little shake, removes the wire, and twists off the cork, aiming, naturally, for a quiet corner of the ceiling. In fact, the bottle is slippery—the cork defiant—and it blasts forth with a thrust that would delight the computers at Cape Canaveral, destroying the chandelier, ricocheting off the armoire, and sending at least one merrymaker to the ophthalmologist. On other occasions it has been known to drill a neat bore through the center of a hanging Renoir and to knock an Archipenko six feet from its base.

It also discharges a small geyser of foam and gas, releasing bubbles that were meant to stay in the wine instead of staining the tablecloth.

Of course, the emerging wine snob, anxious for his moment on stage, argues that Champagne, without popping the cork, is the Fourth of July without fireworks. Maturity, or a couple of lawsuits, may calm him down. Wine snobbery does suggest showmanship, but not assault with a deadly weapon.

The fashionable and aristocratic approach is to determine the perfect moment, when everybody is standing around, and then bring forth the bottle. Everyone will expect the cork to fly, but instead you discreetly wrap a small towel around the neck and cork, smiling here and there, and generally acting witty and urbane. The crowd, having gathered to see *Gunfight at the O.K. Corral,* will be surprised when Fred Astaire appears, and although disappointed, will stay tuned in.

You grip the cork with your hand underneath the towel, and twist the bottle with your other hand. The cork will release and fly into the netting of the towel. There will be no applause but much astonishment. So *that's* the way to open a Champagne bottle! they will think. Of course they will pretend they knew all along. Snobbery is not the exclusive privilege of the wine drinker.

THE CEREMONY OF THE CORK
Part II

The controversy over corks is not limited to Champagne bottles. You are at this pleasant French restaurant, and you order a bottle of Château Meyney 1975. The waiter uncorks the bottle with considerable fanfare and some movements not generally observed outside of the American Ballet Theatre. He places the cork on the table in front of you. Do you smell it, squeeze it, read it, or ignore it?

Well, apparently you don't ignore it because otherwise why would he put it there? That leaves three choices:

DO YOU SMELL IT? There are various reasons why you do not smell it, the first and most obvious being: Why smell it if you're about to taste it? The second reason is that unless you are a professional it is difficult to judge intelligently by smelling the cork. Yes, if the wine has turned to vinegar it will show, but if the wine is simply a little acidic it will not be detectable. The last reason you should not smell it is that it is an unpleasant thing to do. The cork is ugly, the gesture is ugly, and the whole idea borders on the vulgar.

Do not for a moment suppose that sniffing the cork is one of those elegant and knowledgeable demonstrations that indicate some standing in the community of wine snobbery. Some rules for wine snobs are the same as for ordinary people: If it doesn't make sense don't do it.

Do you squeeze it? You don't squeeze a cork for the same reason you don't smell it: You can't judge the wine. There are firm, rubbery corks that have bottled acid, and there are some old, dark, crumbly corks that have protected magnificent wine. It is true that a wine can be spoiled by a dried-out cork, which is why bottles should be stored on their sides. But if the wine is bad, squeezing the cork will not tell you so.

There's another reason why you shouldn't squeeze the cork: It's messy. Who would want to?

Do you read it? Well, you *can* read a cork, although it does demand pretty good vision. These days I have enough trouble reading the menu. Still, it *is* possible, and the good bottles have their names and vintages burned into the cork. Of course they also have their names on the label, which presumably the waiter has already presented. So now the only reason to read the cork would be to *confirm* the label; to ensure that a mediocre bottle of wine did not get an expensive label pasted on. It has happened, but we are now into forgery. To police the wine industry goes beyond the duty of the wine snob.

All right, we don't smell, squeeze or read the cork. What *do* we do? The answer is: Since there is nothing sensible to do, we do nothing. If the waiter delays pouring, waiting for you to do *something* with the cork, simply move it to the side or place it in the ashtray. That may suggest that you don't want the damn thing, and an alert waiter will quickly remove it. The truth is he doesn't know what you're supposed to do with it either.

I've asked a dozen waiters why they present the cork and they all mumble something about "the way it's done," or "our customers expect it." In fact, nobody expects it, nobody wants it, and everybody is made uncomfortable by it.

Presenting the cork is wine nonsense, a ritual invented by waiters and sommeliers. The wine snob doesn't resent ritual. There is infinite ritual in the etiquette of serving wine. But most of it at least *hints* at style or purpose. Placing an unsightly cork on the tablecloth hints at absurdity.

The wine snob—neither a leader of movements nor a revolutionary—need not *confront* the waiter over the cork ceremony, but neither should he participate. Indeed, a mild show of disdain—a wrinkling of the nose that says, "Get this wretched thing out of here!"—seems obligatory.

SURVIVING
THE BLIND
TASTING

As the bankruptcy courts are overflowing with adventurers, confident they could beat the tables in Las Vegas, and the bodies were piled high in Dodge City of cowboys who tried to draw on Wyatt Earp, so the graveyard of wine snobbery is filled with the daring who thought they could guess the wine blindfolded.

It is to wine tasting as the fast draw was to gunfighting, as the no-hitter is to baseball and the hole in one is to golf: the single classic performance. It has that stature—that shade of nobility: a single flourish by which we shall distinguish the master.

Naturally, the wine snob dreams about the moment when he will be asked to identify the wine. The room becomes silent as the wine is poured. The wine snob holds the glass between thumb and forefinger, lowering it to the white tablecloth to judge the intensity of color. Then he swirls it gently, brings it to his nose and tastes it very, very slowly. All this is happening in his dream—a dream replayed in the Betamax of his mind as Babe Ruth must have replayed the sixtieth home run.

The pronouncement follows, with appropriate reserve and just the merest hint of arrogance. "I think it must be a Bordeaux, probably a Margaux. It is certainly not in the class of Château Margaux, and yet it's quite a distinguished wine. I think I'll guess Château Prieuré-Lichine. The year? 1974."

The room remains hushed. The towel is removed from the bottle. It is Prieuré-Lichine 1974. There is much astonishment and light clapping.

That is the fantasy of the wine snob, and like all fantasies it affords hours of pleasure. But sadly, it has never happened. Any expert will concede that it is virtually impossible.

It's urgent that the wine snob realize this, because otherwise he will one day offer to guess a bottle blind, and his performance will become one of the best-loved wine stories in America.

"You say he guessed Prieuré-Lichine 1974? And what was it?"

"A Cabernet from Argentina."

"Oh my goodness."

Thus it is imperative for those who aspire to the Round Table of wine snobbery: Never attempt to guess a wine blind.

It's unlikely for at least four reasons:

1. The possibilities are endless. Even if you are able to determine that it is a red Bordeaux, there are hundreds of châteaux and dozens of years.

2. Even if you know what a Prieuré-Lichine 1974 tastes like, there are variables that could cause it to taste different. How well was it stored? How long was it uncorked? Sometimes a '74 Prieuré-Lichine doesn't taste like a '74 Prieuré-Lichine.

3. The host, who is offering the test, might choose an atypical bottle. You are going to guess Prieuré-Lichine 1974, and he is going to uncover a label from South Africa.

4. It's more difficult to guess a wine than we think. We are served a '74 Prieuré-Lichine in a restaurant, and we agree this is what the wine should taste like. We forget that we are predisposed: We already *know* what the wine is. When a bottle is tasted blind the circumstances are dramatically different.

The Wine and Food Society has arranged events

during which wine was served without identification. The guesses were always disastrous. In fact, if we so much as identified it correctly as an Italian *white*—forget about Soave, Frascati or Verdicchio—that was a good result. And this was The Wine and Food Society, so there were experts among the crowd, or at least people professing to be.

It can't be done, wine snobs of America; it can't be done. And if you are going to stake your reputation on a blind-tasting performance, you will become another statistic in the graveyard.

Well then, what to do? After all, you might be invited to a blind tasting. How to handle it?

There is really one classic rule: *Don't try to be smart. Do try to avoid looking stupid.* If you guess a wine to be a '74 Prieuré-Lichine, you can't avoid looking stupid. That guess has about the same chance of winning as a lottery ticket. Given a wine that suggests a '74 Prieuré-Lichine, identify it as a Bordeaux of a reasonably good year, not in the class of Margaux or Latour but from a perfectly respectable vineyard. If you even get that close you will be doing very nicely.

If you feel that level of identification is not much of an accomplishment, let me tell you that at a recent blind tasting at the Pen and Pencil restaurant in New York, six fairly knowledgeable wine enthusiasts were identifying bottles, and the six identifications usually included six countries, and often more than one continent. The best guess of the evening correctly identified a bottle as "a red Bordeaux from an off year." It was the best guess, not because it was so precise, but because the other five guesses on the same bottle included Burgundy, California, Italy, Spain and Australia. Australia was me.

Identifying wines blind is a little like playing golf. Try to keep your ball on the fairway and forget about the hole in one.

Another good rule to follow is to sit next to an expert. Don't be intimidated: Sitting next to an expert will not place demands on you. The demands are on him and he knows how to handle them. All eyes will sweep right by you, focusing on him, anxious to hear the prediction. And so, as the wine is tasted, you will be *expected* to defer—to turn toward your expert and ask, "What do you think?"

Nobody expects a wine taster sitting next to Peter Sichel to venture a guess, any more than one would expect someone sitting next to Henry Kissinger to comment on foreign policy.

You can get through this thing reputation intact. It's not easy. This is not the minor leagues; this is the World Series of wine expertise. But you don't have to point to the bleachers and hit a home run. Try for a single, but most of all, don't strike out.

AT THE CATHEDRAL OF WINE SNOBBERY

The education and refinement of a wine snob require a visit to one of the elegant wineries of the world, because one day you will be sipping Port and someone will ask, "Have you ever visited Oporto?"

Of course that is not really a question. The translation is "I've visited Oporto, and I assume you haven't." Clearly there's a new gunfighter in town.

There are always new gunfighters, just as there were in Dodge City, and they always have a new trick or a different angle. This one has "Oporto," and he's come to town thinking he might draw against Château Lafite. Well, Oporto is to wine snobbery as a local cowboy might be to Wyatt Earp. With Oporto as his weapon he is headed for the wine snobbery graveyard. Oh yes, he might get a little attention, but when Wyatt Earp walks through the swinging barroom doors our local hero better get the hell out of there. So much for Oporto. The question is, Which winery is to wine snobbery as Wyatt Earp is to gunfighting? The answer is Château d'Yquem.

Certainly there are others. Chambertin would be quite distinguished; Romanée-Conti would be unchallengeable. But there is a curious elegance—a patina—to Château d'Yquem, and when you're packing Yquem in your holster you can walk through the swinging doors and watch the local pretenders scatter.

Which may explain why Rita and I (one wine snob, one suffering wife) left the town of Bordeaux one morning at ten, driving toward Sauternes.

As the lover of Shakespeare makes his pilgrimage to Stratford-on-Avon, and the Renaissance scholar journeys to Florence, the wine snob knows that sooner or later he must visit Sauternes. And the jewel of Sauternes—the perfect emerald in the perfect setting—is Château d'Yquem.

Sauternes is a region as the Médoc is a region or the Napa Valley is a region. Within each of those boundaries are found wineries, producing a characteristic wine (or wines of different character). Sauternes produces a sweet white wine that is rarely ordered with dinner. It is called a dessert wine.

I think it only fair to mention that Rita felt that a visit to Château d'Yquem was something less than a pilgrimage and not at all essential to protecting my reputation as a wine snob. I pointed out the new gunfighters in town—I mentioned Oporto. She remained indifferent. The education and refinement of a wine snob require a supportive spouse, and it doesn't hurt if she's something of a snob herself. Rita's no snob, which may explain why my standing in the world of wine snobbery is not quite as exalted as it might be.

But anyway, she agreed to come along, and that's worth something. So there we were, driving south, carefully following directions given to us at the hotel. It's not difficult to locate the region of Sauternes, and I was certain that once there we could find the château. I assumed it would be like asking a Parisian where the Eiffel Tower was. After all, I was asking about Yquem, one of the world's most glorious wines.

It is not quite as easy as that, but I was finally able to get help from the proprietor of a nearby restaurant, the Auberge des Vignes, who told me that it was not more than a mile away.

"There are signs," I said. I didn't *ask* because of course there had to be signs and I didn't want to appear stupid. There had to be signs to Yquem as there have to be signs to Chartres, to Versailles—to Paris even.

"There are no signs," he said.

I can assure you he's right about that. We didn't even know we were at Château d'Yquem even after we arrived. We were later to learn that so many tourists want to visit Yquem that it far exceeds their capacity and they try to remain somewhat hidden. Well, all the better for wine snobbery.

It was late October, past the tourist season, and it hadn't occurred to me to make an appointment. Concerned that I might be turned away (how could I ever explain *that?*), I set about finding someone who looked reasonably important. That's not easy to do. In wine country, when they are pressing the grapes, everyone wears dungarees and chinos, and miserable-looking chinos at that. But I finally found the right person, and after some desperate pleading he agreed to give us a tour at two-thirty. It was noon; time for lunch.

It's fortunate that the Auberge des Vignes was only a mile away because I don't know how I would have otherwise convinced Rita to hang around for two and a half hours. But Rita is vulnerable in the food department although I might have taken some advantage in telling her that—although I wasn't certain—I thought the restaurant had two stars in *Michelin*. She didn't need much encouragement; if food snobbery ever reaches the heights of wine snobbery, it will be difficult putting up with her.

We started lunch with a half bottle of Sauternes, Château Rieussec 1976. It was the first and probably the last time I *begin* lunch with a Sauternes. The wine is simply too sweet. There are wine enthusiasts, particularly from the region of Sauternes, who feel that the wine is appropriate at any stage of dining, but most wine lovers disagree. Today, however, we had just passed Château Rieussec on the road and it seemed like something we ought to do. Besides, you never know when—back home in Dodge City—you can casually mention, "We started lunch with a Sauternes." Raised eyebrows, everywhere.

We shared two dishes for lunch: lamproie à la bordelaise and salmis de cailles. The first is a gamy fish, caught in the local waters and prepared in a dark-red wine sauce, a specialty of the region. Cailles are quail, and our dish was prepared in a Sauternes sauce. Both dishes were excellent, and the restaurant is a perfect choice when you spend a day in Sauternes country.

It was near two-thirty and we returned to Château d'Yquem. Our guide was Pierre Meslier, the general manager. Usually when one arranges a tour of a château, there is a student guide. One doesn't get taken around by the general manager because general managers have other things to do. I think it must have been my discerning eye and grand demeanor.

The moment was perfect. The trucks were driving in from the fields with wooden buckets full of grapes, and the grapes were being unloaded into a hopper where the crushing operation begins.

In Sauternes, the harvesting and pressing of the grapes has one highly unusual characteristic: The grapes are left on the vine until they are attacked by a parasite. It is called the pourriture noble, the noble rot. The rot appears in the late summer and covers the grape with a grey mold, cracking the skin and allowing the water in the juice to evaporate. The result is a shriveled, purple-gray cross between a grape and a raisin. Until it reaches that state of rot it remains on the vine. A single cluster of grapes hanging from the vine will have individual grapes in every condition from perfect to rotted, and so they must be individually picked. It requires that the pickers go through the vineyards perhaps ten times, an expense that contributes to the high cost of Château d'Yquem and to all fine Sauternes.

The story of this curious method of making wine goes back to the year 1847. The Marquis de Lur-Saluces, the owner of Château d'Yquem, was away in Russia, having left instructions that the harvest not begin until he returned. But his return was delayed and on his arrival the grapes had turned overripe and been attacked by rot. Having little choice he harvested and pressed the grapes anyway, and they resulted in a wine that was extraordinary. So at Château d'Yquem, more than a century afterwards, each summer they await with pleasure the arrival of the noble rot.

After the grapes are crushed they are tested for sugar content and then pressed in three large wooden presses. The juice is then run off into oak barrels where the fermentation begins. If you put your ear to the opening in the top of the barrel you can hear the bubbling as yeast turns the sugar into alcohol—the essential process by which all wine is made.

I think I ought to admit that I was doing my best to impress Mr. Meslier with my knowledge of wine and my standing in the wine community. Rita would later tell me that I was pompous at best and insufferable at worst, a criticism I completely reject on the grounds that she knows almost nothing about wine. And anyway, so what if I mentioned a fact or two to my friend Pierre Meslier? What are we to talk about in this very cathedral of the wine industry?

As Pierre Meslier showed us through the wine-making operation at Château d'Yquem, we were amazed at the simple equipment that produces this extraordinary wine. We had visited châteaux that produce red Bordeaux—Château Mouton-Rothschild, Château Palmer, Château Lynch-Bages—each of them equipped with huge 20-foot fermentation tanks, modern winepresses and a network of pipes and conveyors. At Yquem there is a single hopper, about the size of a wooden barrel, that receives and crushes all the grapes from the vineyard. Directly behind the hopper stand three wooden presses, resembling oversized barrels. That's all there is. From there the juice is piped into oak casks for fermentation, and finally, three years later, it is bottled. The explanation for these surprisingly limited facilities—one has no sense of a grand wine in the making—is that Yquem is picked grape by grape, then picked again and again as the grapes rot, and the flow of grapes never exceeds the capacity of the equipment. Simple and sensible.

It was exciting to be with Mr. Meslier, a man

presiding over the making of perhaps the world's greatest white wine, and when the tour was over he invited us into the tasting room where he poured two glasses of 1975 Yquem.

Now this is an important moment in the life of any wine enthusiast: to drink Yquem at the château, and with Pierre Meslier. I was already contemplating how I might appropriately understate it at the next meeting of The Wine and Food Society.

"It was only a modest 1975."

"Pierre Meslier brought out a special bottle . . ."

"My friend, Pierre . . ."

And of course I hadn't tasted the wine yet. This is a moment for reverence. Perhaps twenty minutes of heady wine discussion should precede the tasting. So I asked Pierre about his favorite vintages and I asked Pierre what was the oldest bottle of Yquem he had tasted (1861). And I swirled the wine around the glass and sniffed and held it to the light, remarking about the color. I had the feeling that Pierre was extremely impressed, and I put the glass to my lips, turning just slightly to Rita to be certain she was following accepted procedure. A moment of profound horror overcame me; her glass was empty. Could Meslier have failed to serve her? Impossible. Could Rita have gulped a glass of Château d'Yquem?

Indeed it had happened. Unable to restrain herself through a mere twenty minutes of illuminating analysis of the noble rot, Rita had committed the ultimate heresy. The story would circulate immediately, crisscrossing Europe and hopping the next plane to New York. I would be the target of every gunfighter between Taillevent and Lutèce.

Fully expecting it to be reported in *Time* magazine, I was relieved to see the cover story was Ronald Reagan. Nevertheless, I always sit facing the swinging doors, with my right hand on the pearl handle.

THE RASPBERRY SAUCE CONTROVERSY

The wine snob is expected to know about food, and is expected to have his culinary recommendations confirmed in the highest places. He is also expected to discover the three-star restaurants before they are given three stars. The wine snob who recommended La Tulipe or Dodin-Bouffant before they blossomed in Mimi Sheraton's column had his reputation ensured.

Conversely, the wine snob is expected to be aware of those restaurants on the decline. It is an embarrassment of stunning proportions to be known around town as a devotee of some grand establishment that Sheraton, on Friday morning, drops to one star. The best response is to spend the weekend in the Catskills and to accept no calls.

It's rather an unfair burden to keep up with the restaurant scene when you are, at the same time, trying to sort out a hundred small wineries in the state of California. Nevertheless it must be done; the wine snob who does not read Sheraton on Friday might just as well take up origami.

Nor does it end with Sheraton. The most comprehensive listing of the Manhattan culinary scene is found in *The Restaurants of New York* by Seymour Britchky. Seymour (the wine snob calls all restaurant reviewers by their first names) also has a star system, but not necessarily conforming to Mimi's. In fact, on such established Manhattan restaurants as The Palm and The Coach House, they are in enemy camps.

Mimi (giving The Coach House four stars): "The velvety black bean soup is a house classic."

Seymour (giving The Coach House no stars): "The famous black bean soup is sometimes claylike, sometimes tepid, sometimes both, no match for certain Cuban soups around town."

The wine snob is obliged to walk the gastronomic tightrope between Sheraton and Britchky—always in balance, never falling, because indeed there is no net. You might want to try the black bean soup at The Coach House, but it would always be *in spite of* what Seymour had to say about it.

It also doesn't hurt to be aware of *Forbes* magazine's annual listing of New York's best restaurants, although the correct approach is to treat the listing with disdain and a general air of "What can the business community know about fine food?" Whether *Forbes* is on or off target, your attitude will be respected. Nobody loves General Motors.

In an expansive mood you might even take a passing shot at the *Forbes* list:

"*Forbes?* Doesn't Malcolm still give '21' Club four stars?"

That should do it. Nobody loves the "21" Club either, except maybe the vice-presidents of General Motors, who are not regarded as aficionados of dining, and lately, not even of automobiles.

Of course, it's also necessary to stay informed about the restaurant *specialties:*

"Sweetbreads? You must try them at Mon Paris. They prepare them braised in an almost-sweet chestnut sauce."

"You're going to Patsy's? Ask them to prepare a side order of string beans marinara."

"Surely you're not comparing any cheesecake in New York to the one served at Grotta Azzurra."

Stuff like that.

It even involves sauces. In fact it most definitely

involves sauces. We were with Reginald one evening recently at Lutèce. We never go to Lutèce
without Reginald because it's his favorite restaurant
and he has committed the menu to memory. This is
one of the great accomplishments in wine and food
snobbery because a person would deserve a good
deal of respect if he so much as *understood* the
Lutèce menu. Reginald's dedication has not gone
unnoticed by André Soltner, who stops at our table
to discuss the special preparations of the evening,
occasionally bringing along some mousse of pigeon.

At the time of this dinner there was a considerable flap about the two sauces served with the roast
duck; Sheraton, I believe, having advised against
the raspberry sauce. Well now, this was a major
event in the kingdom of snobbery. *Everyone* was
aware that you order the duckling at Lutèce à
l'orange.

Roger, the waiter, was taking the orders, and
Reginald in fact ordered duck.

"Orange or raspberry sauce?" asked Roger.

I smiled to myself. Here I am sitting next to one of America's distinguished wine and food snobs, presiding over a delicate decision, but certain to handle it correctly—*certain* to order duck à l'orange.

"What do you suggest, Roger?" asked Reginald.

I was shocked; apparently Reginald didn't know about the raspberry sauce. Someone at the next table might overhear this. Someone might actually *see* Roger ladling raspberry sauce over our duck.

"Have the raspberry sauce," counseled Roger.

There it goes, I thought. The sinking of the *Titanic*; the explosion of the *Hindenburg*.

Reginald nodded. Roger smiled broadly.

I was having cassolette de crabe and hiding behind my menu, fighting to preserve my own reputation as the walls of wine snobbery were caving in around me.

The entrées were served and I did notice that Roger was being especially gracious. When we ordered a Château Simard '73 he said, "I think I can find you a '70; we have one or two bottles left."

It was only toward the end of dinner that I found the courage to ask Reginald about the duck, and I asked the question casually—without reference to the raspberry sauce. Reginald was about to be drummed out of the battalion; no sense adding to his misery.

"Do you mean," he said, "why did I not order it à l'orange right away?"

"Well, I didn't mean to question you, Reginald, but since you ask . . ."

"Nobody with any background at all would order the duck à l'orange. It would be an insult."

"But . . ."

"To order the duck à l'orange would be to acknowledge, at America's finest restaurant—where, incidentally, I am regarded as a patron with some knowledge of wine and food—that the raspberry sauce was inadequate. And why? Because Mimi said so? Surely we listen to Mimi on the restaurants around town, and we might be influenced by an innovative preparation she suggested at Lutèce. But we do not—we absolutely do not—*avoid* a preparation. Who knows why Mimi didn't like the raspberry sauce? The point is, it was prepared by André Soltner."

Reginald was in fine form and there was no stopping him. "Now, if someone prefers an orange sauce with duck he might order it. But if you or I ordered it—given that we've read the review—it would be in incredibly bad taste. Clearly we order duck, and we leave the rest to Roger."

"But what did you *think* of the raspberry sauce?" I asked, hanging on the edge of the cliff by my fingernails.

Reginald turned to me with an imperious air, shaded, I thought, by just a touch of pity. "It simply doesn't matter a bit what I think," he said.

I wasn't invited to the next two Lutèce dinners, appropriate punishment for a performance bordering on the barbarian. And certainly my standing on the ladder of wine snobbery has slipped a few levels—not that it was so high to begin with.

Reginald, of course, remains on top—knowledgeable about wine, knowledgeable about food—ever alert, ever discreet, always correct.

A
MOMENT
OF TRIUMPH

I slipped into a serious depression over the raspberry sauce incident, and wondered how I might effect a recovery. Finally I decided that four days in Paris was the only approach.

Paris is, to the wine snob, as Florence is to the Renaissance scholar: essential. As Florence houses the art treasures of the fourteenth and fifteenth centuries: Giotto, Fra Angelico, Botticelli—Paris boasts the gastronomic treasures of the twentieth: Taillevent, Faugeron, L'Archestrate. Some may feel that this comparison is strained, pointing to a certain qualitative difference between the Botticelli "Primavera" and the rack of lamb at Taillevent. Never mind about that: Those people will never succeed as wine snobs.

The restaurants of Paris are household words in the language of wine snobbery, but it's important to echo the prevailing sentiment: that the grand three-star establishments have deteriorated. To return from Paris and discourse enthusiastically about Tour d'Argent or Vivarois is an error of almost unrecoverable proportions.

On the other hand, to return from Paris and drop a name or two that nobody has yet heard does your standing little harm. My own standing, after Lutèce, could suffer little harm in any case.

So I booked for Paris and spent a solid week researching the restaurants and wine lists, including a call to my friend Charles, who represents a group owning a vineyard in the Rhone Valley. Charles is not a wine snob, simply because he does not choose to be one. Given his background and knowledge I regard it as a serious error of judgment.

Charles recommended, among other restaurants, Le Pré Catelan, and I added it to my list, cross-checking with *Michelin*—although not very carefully with a recommendation from such an impeccable source.

Rita and I arrived at the restaurant. (Rita claims that my dedication to wine snobbery is superficial and indulgent, although she seems to endure the grand restaurants of Paris with hardly a whimper.) We were seated, ordered the house apéritif: Champagne with fresh raspberries, and asked for the wine list.

There is a notion, entertained by those who have not visited Paris, that French wine is less expensive in France. The idea is not unreasonable, but quite the opposite is true. As I considered the red Bordeaux of the type I might order at home, I noted that Château Talbot and Château Ducru-Beaucaillou, both 1970s, were £17. Château Gloria 1970 was £15, and Château Léoville-Las-Cases 1973 (a good but undistinguished year) was £35. They were all wines which might have been found on a list in New York or Chicago at that time for £10.

As my eye traveled farther down the list I found a Grand-Puy-Lacoste 1960, and the price was £12. It was the cheapest red Bordeaux on the list, clearly an indication that the house had little confidence in the bottle.

Certain things need to be said about Grand-Puy-Lacoste and the year 1960. First, the château is underrated; second, the year 1960 is considerably underrated, sandwiched between two of the greatest vintages of the century, 1959 and 1961; and third, the wine comes from the district of Pauillac—the district that gives us Château Lafite-Rothschild, Château Mouton-Rothschild and Château Latour—

a district known for the long-lasting character of its wines. A Grand-Puy-Lacoste 1960 could be a magnificent bottle of wine.

I pointed it out to the waiter, suggesting that it seemed like a promising bottle, certainly considering the price. He shook his head solemnly. "A good price, yes, but the year—1960. I couldn't recommend it."

"Have you served a bottle?"

"No, I don't remember a bottle being served."

Now this was something of a confrontation. One does not, in the great restaurants of Paris, disregard the waiter's recommendation. I could imagine a most unpleasant situation arising as the bottle was opened and the wine was flat or acidic. But I could also see unfolding a ticker-tape parade down the Champs Elysées if I was correct. Had I not manhandled the raspberry sauce incident I might not have gambled, but I had little to lose and I needed a victory.

"I'll try it," I said.

The waiter did not seem happy, but he nodded and hurried off to bring the bottle from the cellar. It was probably true that he hadn't served it before because it took him twenty minutes to find it.

It is understood that the wine snob does not order the most expensive bottle on the list, or the cheapest, or the most reliable. He searches for the unique, the most interesting, the most promising bottle at the price. Here was a bottle that the very establishment at one of Paris's most elegant restaurants had turned their backs on—that they wouldn't even recommend—an outcast. That is always of more than passing interest to the wine snob.

The waiter poured the wine with appropriate ceremony, and I tasted it. It was remarkable—not only good but outstanding—better than I might even have hoped. It was soft and yet intense; the twenty years of aging had brought it to a marvelous perfection.

My waiter was standing by and another waiter had joined him awaiting the verdict on this curious bottle. To nod approval would have been hopelessly inadequate.

"Taste it," I said.

He did, and he was astonished, so I insisted that the other waiter taste it as well. They both smiled broadly and raised their glasses in appreciation and respect. It was a glorious moment in the life of a wine snob—a genuine triumph.

I returned to New York and could hardly wait to arrange dinner with Reginald, at which time this story would be told with suitable modesty and reserve, preferably at a table with not less than eight serious wine people. Of course I would have to be careful. One doesn't dramatize the already dramatic.

Dinner for two at Le Pré Catelan was £80—a high price to pay for a few rungs on the ladder.

Not too high, I thought.

SENDING BACK
THE BOTTLE

Attention, wine snobs in training: This is the chapter you've been waiting for. This is the chapter on SENDING BACK THE BOTTLE. Don't deny it—you've been anticipating the moment. Surrounded by admiring friends, the waiter opens a '78 Sancerre. You taste it; it's a bit acidic—a bit, what shall we say, off-balance. Certainly not what a Sancerre should be. It appears that the moment has arrived.

The table is awaiting your approval. You put the glass down, then pick it up and taste again. Apparently there's a problem. Some friends at the table shift nervously. The waiter clears his throat. You signal with your hand as though you were brushing away a fly: The wine is unacceptable. One or two friends are hiding behind their menus. There is a light cough from the far end of the table. The waiter questions you politely, but not without an edge of disbelief. You taste again, but the wine is simply not good and the bottle is sent back. The wine snob has played his most demanding role.

Or has he? Has he played Hamlet, or has he played the Fool?

Somewhere it is written that sending-back-the-bottle is the grand gesture of wine snobbery. Actually it's the grand gesture of silliness, and the reason is not difficult to understand. All kinds of show-offs and buffoons send back perfectly sound bottles for no other reason than to appear knowledgeable. So badly is this practice abused that it is now difficult to send back a *bad* bottle. The sender immediately joins the theatre of the absurd.

It is therefore necessary to consider when the wine gets sent back, and also how to do it without making everyone uncomfortable for the rest of the evening.

THE BAD BOTTLE

A bad bottle always goes back, simply because it is not drinkable. Usually it has a sour taste—more than a hint of acid. There is no reason to suffer through such a bottle so you call the waiter and tell him. Waiters are not known for their charm and graciousness in such circumstances, but you're not at the restaurant to please the waiter. He's there to please you. Or at least that's the way it's supposed to be.

The waiter will taste it and either replace it without comment or advise you that there's nothing wrong with it. That's always a problem although fortunately a rare one. If it happens you might say:

"We have all tasted the wine and nobody at the table thinks it's sound, but if you're certain it is, please ask the owner to come to the table and taste it. If he says there is nothing wrong we will keep it."

This serves the purpose of advising the waiter that you are not the only one dissatisfied and that you are not playing the send-back-the-bottle game. If he persists he is challenging the judgment of four or six customers. Only the stubborn will persist.

Alas, there are some waiters who will still challenge you, and that is why you ask—albeit politely—for the owner. That request suggests to the waiter that even if *he* is willing to offend everyone at the table, perhaps the owner will think differently about it. The chances are favorable that the waiter will take the bottle rather than bring the owner, but even if he does bring the owner, it's O.K. Owners have more pride in their restaurants and their reputations than waiters do. Owners,

generally, won't lie about something as trivial as a bottle of wine.

If he does lie then my suggestion proves worthless. Put aside the bottle, order another one, and scratch the restaurant from your list. You've done the best you can.

There are those who will argue that this approach is too passive. Why ask anyone? they insist. If the wine is bad send it back, and if the waiter objects send it back anyway.

But now dinner has become a pitched battle. The waiter is at best coldly polite. You and your friends are at best irritated and anxious. It seems like an unpleasant way to spend two hours in a restaurant. A bit of diplomacy works better.

THE WRONG YEAR

This depends on the type of wine.

The year is quite important in French wines, France being subject to every kind of climatic uncertainty. It either rains too much or too little in Burgundy and Bordeaux, causing the price of the '75s to be twice that of the '73s. If you order a '75 you should get a '75.

In Italian, Spanish and Portuguese wines the year is not terribly important and the restaurant is not as dedicated to the accuracy of its wine list as in French restaurants. Mama is in the kitchen stirring the marinara sauce, and Papa is running around among the tables. Who has time to keep an up-to-date wine list? If you order a '75 and they bring a

'76, it probably means they ran out of the '75s. Since it is unlikely that the difference will be significant, keep the wine.

In American and also German wines the year is *moderately* important. Here you might judge by price. If you are paying nine pounds for a German Wehlener Sonnenuhr 1976 you should get the year you are paying for. If the bottle is a four-pound Leibfraumilch and they bring a different year, you should keep it.

THE WRONG ATTITUDE

We're dining at L'Epicure and have ordered a 1970 Calon-Ségur. The waiter brings the bottle and opens it: The label reads 1971. There is no reason to keep the bottle. If the waiter wished to make an alternative suggestion—if he had said, "We're out of the '70 but I think you'll enjoy the '71 just as much"—that's one thing. But simply to open the '71 without approval is indifferent and almost arrogant.

Don't ever believe that you must defer to the waiter or wine-waiter. A good restaurant always regards your choice with respect. At Lutèce, recently, I ordered a vintage Port after dessert and my friend ordered a Cognac. We both asked which bottles they intended to serve, and the waiter responded by bringing both bottles to the table.

Although there is no excuse for an arrogant waiter, it's important to understand the restaurant's point of view. They are all a little shell-shocked from customers who believe that it is a sign of sophistication to send back the bottle. Their first reaction to a rejected bottle is to suspect the customer and not the wine.

So remember, you can swirl and sniff, clear your palate, and goodness knows you can carry on a little. But sending back the bottle is another matter. Hard cash is involved here. There are stages on which the theatre of wine snobbery may be played with all the grandeur of King Lear, but this is not one of them. And to play Lear when the staging calls for Puck is one of the great embarrassments of Broadway, Off Broadway or anywhere else.

THE SUMMER WINE TASTING

My friend Marvin is a dilettante. By day he flits around between the Stock Exchange and the tennis courts—never in either place long enough to get a hold of him—and by evening he visits the latest SoHo gallery or boutique restaurant. I've always known that sooner or later Marvin would decide to become a wine snob.

"Introduce me to Reginald," Marvin said one day, to nobody's surprise.

There can be only one reason why anyone would want to meet Reginald: to become a wine snob. He is totally uninterested in any subject other than wine. An evening with Reginald is an evening spent discussing rainfall levels in the Rhone Valley, all of the discussing being carried on by Reginald since he and the weatherman at Châteauneuf-du-Pape are the only two people in the world who know about stuff like that.

A few of Marvin's tennis buddies, taking Adult Education courses in wine tasting, have been dropping château names on him lately, unnerving Marvin terribly. So Marvin decided that he must not only learn about wine, but learn to affect the proper demeanor. Of course that requires an introduction to the high priest of the wine community. I arranged for them to have lunch, and Reginald called me afterwards.

"It's hopeless," he said. "Marvin buys his suits at Alexander's."

"He'll change," I answered. "Marvin wants to be a wine snob and he has the time and money to accomplish it."

There was a long pause. I guessed I had said the wrong thing. It's easy to say the wrong things when talking to Reginald.

"I don't think you understand," said Reginald. "It has very little to do with money."

As a personal favor to me Reginald finally allowed that if Marvin would consider a new wardrobe and generally keep his mouth shut in the company of wine people, Reginald would tentatively accept him as a hanger-on. We would then see if Marvin showed any promise, and if he did we would move him up.

This was agreed to, and Marvin became a wine-snob-in-training, which, under the tutelage of Reginald, might be like studying the piano under Rubinstein.

Marvin learned twirling and sniffing, clearing the palate and decanting, and generally dispatched himself creditably, although without particular style or panache. He made up in determination what he lacked in flair, and little by little he was working his way into the group, even to the point of being included in a dinner at Chanterelle, the understanding being that his rightful place at the table would be as far away from Reginald as possible.

In spite of that, Marvin was handed the wine list that evening and asked to select the wine for the first course. We were all having sweetbreads. He chose, apparently to the surprise of Reginald, a Pouilly-Fuissé—1978. This was of course a critical moment, and I could tell from Reginald's expression that he was not at all disappointed.

A week later Reginald called me. "Let's invite him to the next Wine and Food Society tasting," he said.

I could hardly wait to call Marvin. "Do you know what this means? This means you've been accepted."

It might be helpful to explain that Reginald and Marvin are at opposite ends of the personality scale. Marvin is friendly and agreeable, always smiling, always having fun. Some of us feel that in his almost single-minded pursuit of fun he has allowed his brain to get a little moldy. He is not the one to contact if you are in the mood to discuss Kierkegaard. Of course, if you *are* in the mood to discuss Kierkegaard, I don't know that you are offered a wide range of possibilities. Marvin looks and acts like a smaller Maurice Chevalier, ebullient, ruddy, ever optimistic. If things get tough in the stock market, Marvin could get a cane and a bowler and audition for a 1920s musical.

Reginald, on the other hand, is somber. Somber may even have been *coined* to describe Reginald. Impeccably dressed in deep grey or black, he could fit unobtrusively into a Charles Addams cartoon. His eyes sink deep, skeletonlike, in the sockets; his mouth is a slash, his complexion damp. He has a way of staring at you while you're explaining something that convinces you you're wrong. And since you're generally explaining something about wine—that being all Reginald will listen to—you probably are.

Obviously he is demanding, impatient, arrogant and intolerant. Such a figure we have elected to be leader of the wine snob fraternity.

So I was less than confident about the forthcoming tasting, where Reginald and Marvin would sit together. Prospects brightened when The Wine and Food Society announced a tasting of "summer" wines, to be held on a cruise ship in New York harbor. It sounded like fun, and it sounded like an event at which Marvin might be comfortable.

"Summer wines" describes light, fruity, chilled wines that are best enjoyed when the weather is warm. Beyond that, there is the understanding that the *rules* are relaxed. You want to drop an ice cube in a glass of Muscadet? O.K. You want to mix a wine cooler with white wine, orange juice and a cherry? O.K. No clearing the palate, no vintage years, no prohibitions. Also no wine snobbery. What's to be snobbish about? Anything goes.

The event was presided over by Peter Sichel, who couples extraordinary knowledge with refreshing good sense. He tapped his glass for silence and began to discuss summer wines. He said, in essence, "Don't be limited by convention. Try new ideas. Have fun."

"Have fun?" asked Marvin.

"Yes," I said, "but remember where you are." I could see that Reginald was not in absolute agreement with Peter about how much fun we were expected to have.

Nevertheless, Marvin rose from the table and immediately proceeded to mix a Vouvray with four fruit juices, a slice of cucumber, a sprig of mint and a maraschino cherry.

"Marvin," I said, "what *is* that?"

"It's everything I could find on tables one and two. And stop looking at me that way. Peter Sichel said ANYTHING GOES. Do you know as much as he does?"

"It looks ridiculous," I said.

"Why don't you taste it."

Everyone at the table was watching me. I tasted it. It was delicious.

"It's fair," I said.

Marvin finished his drink rather quickly. I could see the color rise in his cheeks, and I noted, with some concern, that he was showing little interest in the subject of conversation: whether the 1966 Médocs were maturing better than the 1964s. He left the table again and returned with a highball glass filled with some foaming, flamingo-colored liquid with an orange peel climbing over the top.

"What does it taste like?" I asked foolishly, hoping for an answer that might evidence some restraint.

"To tell you the truth, I love it."

To be fair, it was that kind of an afternoon. The members were drinking various color sensations— many with flowers growing out of the glass. Nor did the conversation remain riveted to the 1960s Médocs.

The person having the best time was Marvin. He was dancing around introducing himself to every-body and drinking his fruit juice concoctions as though they were fruit juice. Everyone thought him jovial and charming up to the very moment when he lifted a straw from his glass and started to lead the band, after which he collapsed slowly into his seat and did not arise.

Reginald and I took him home in a cab, and there was not very much to say. He has not been seen since at The Wine and Food Society, Chanterelle, or anyplace else worth mentioning.

It didn't matter. Marvin had such a good time that he forgot all about sniffing and twirling, forgot all about becoming a wine snob, and took to drinking white wine and orange juice with almost everything.

It mattered only to Reginald, who sponsored him. Reginald was painfully humiliated, and it is well known in wine circles that the subject of Marvin and the Summer Tasting is never to be brought up in his presence.

INSTANT
SNOBBERY

Put yourself in my hands: I have another overnight route to wine snobbery. You needn't learn the vintages or study the rainfall charts. You needn't build a wine cellar or join the Chevaliers du Tastevin. It requires only that you purchase a single bottle of wine, and such a bottle is available. That's the good part.

The bad part is that the wine will cost you some money: It would have to be a bottle from the nineteenth century. There is no denying that a single absolute test of a person's standing in the Hall of Fame of Wine Snobbery is: How old a bottle have you tasted?

I'm sorry about the expense but you can't have everything. This is instant snobbery. You don't have to do anything; you don't have to leave the house. Sherry-Lehmann or D. Sokolin will deliver the bottle to your front door. I'm not sure you even have to taste it. Having it might be enough.

O.K., which bottle do you want? You have choices. The 1858 Lafite-Rothschild will cost you £1,500—probably cheaper by the case. You get a lot of snobbery mileage out of an 1858. Feeling a bit more secure? Buy the 1865 at only £1,200. In a bind? I can get you a special deal. If you act right now—and the price could change at any moment—I can secure you instant snobbery with a bottle of 1893 Château Palmer. Sherry-Lehmann has it on sale for £368. I admit it's not blue-chip snobbery; it's not Lafite or Mouton or Margaux. But it's nineteenth century nevertheless and there are few bottles in the world that can challenge it.

"Is it good to drink?"

How would *I* know? But here's a recent quote from the *Wm. Sokolin Wineletter*:

"I recently decanted a bottle of 1832 Lafite and I sincerely believe it was the finest claret I have ever tasted."

At the same time as I offer you instant wine snobbery, I could be offering almost-instant wealth. Of course I understand that you are above such considerations, so I won't dwell upon the fact that these nineteenth-century bottles have doubled in price during the past year. In any case you can't double your money and at the same time consume the merchandise, a conflict of interest that I trust is not troubling anybody with the nobility of character that would involve him in the pursuit of wine snobbery.

Allow me to mention some approaches that do not qualify. It will not do to purchase an 1865 Lafite and then sell 23 shares at £75 a share. This is good merchandising but it will not go over smoothly at the Chaîne des Rôtisseurs. To taste one/twenty-fourth of a bottle—an ounce of wine—and proclaim that you've tasted the 1865 Lafite is like purchasing a few random pencil lines by Dali and saying you own a Dali. I know you would never consider doing anything like that.

Another approach might be the nineteenth-century Madeiras. They are genuinely old, and lovely besides, but they do not confer instant status. They are reasonably priced—an 1863 Madeira is £68—and reasonably available, but nothing "available" is likely to serve your interests in the rarefied company of nineteenth-century Bordeaux.

Finally you may wish to consider a charity event, and I would hardly want to dissuade you. You purchase an 1822 Lafite for £15,000 (a bottle went for £15,500 at the Heublein auction recently) and donate it to your favorite charity, immediately taking a tax deduction. In the 50 percent bracket this bottle is now costing only £7,500 and is permitting you to help your fellow man as well. Then you plan a party centered around tasting this extraordinary wine, bottled during the lifetime of Thomas Jefferson. For a five-hundred-pound contribution you offer a sip; for two hundred and fifty pounds, a sniff. You invite the governor, the mayor and some local gourmet celebrities, being careful about the latter group as they will expect to taste the wine. The media will cover it—have some beer on hand for them—and you will be deservedly Man of the Year. I caution you to remember, however, that this noble event has to do with charity and not wine snobbery. If you intend to ride your tax deduction into the halls of The Wine and Food Society, you are in for a disappointment. We will applaud your generosity but do not expect our undivided attention when you begin to describe the wine.

Perhaps I'm envious. I've never tasted a wine from the nineteenth century. It has seriously compromised my standing in the wine community and has left me feeling inadequate and defenseless among wine snobs who casually drop into the conversation an 1865 Lafite. Only once in my life did I ever approach tasting a wine of the last century but it eluded my grasp. It was at the 417th meeting of The Wine and Food Society of New York: a comparative tasting of twenty-one vintages of a single château. The oldest bottle was dated 1899.

Such an event is one of the most interesting and informative in the study and appreciation of wine. To make it more remarkable we were to taste Château Latour, one of the five greatest red Bordeaux. Who knows what might be discovered? Perhaps the most intriguing comparison will be between the '64 and the '66. Surely we will discuss the 1970, considering whether it is ready to drink—which it almost certainly will not be. Very likely the great debate will be, Which is the best bottle of the tasting? with a large contingent lining up behind the '59, the '61, and of course the 1899.

Naturally I was lined up behind the 1899, not because of the wine—a bottle that old could be undrinkable—but because of the year. Indeed, because of the century. True, it was only months on the safe side of 1900 but they were precious months, and my guarantee of membership in a most exclusive club.

And then an extraordinary thing happened: As the members set about opening their own particular bottles, nobody approached the 1899. We waited nervously a few moments—a phone call was placed—but it soon became evident that the donor of the 1899 Latour was not at the tasting. Well, now, what to do about *that?* To open the bottle or not?

There I was, with my lifetime reputation almost ensured, not letting the 1899 out of my sight—but where was the donor?

The chairman of the event argued that the bottle should not be opened, and I think it only fair to say that if I had been chairman and had to answer to the donor, I would have argued the same way. The chairman contended that the donor had the right to taste his own wine, that the bottle was irreplaceable, and that it would be discourteous at best to open it in his absence.

So much for the chairman, a man who happens to own one of the major wine collections of the world. What did he know about wine snobbery? What did he know about my sense of urgency—my once-in-a-lifetime chance?

Seizing the moment, I argued strenuously that the donor's obligation was to the event: that the event was the sacred thing. Two or three of the most insecure and snobbish members—their eyes fastened to the 1899 label—rallied to my side, pointing out that if we *did* open it the owner might be disappointed, but if we did not open it the very purpose of the event would be compromised.

Finally someone asked if the donor had called with instructions. He hadn't, and so our group insisted that without advice to the contrary we were free of any obligation not to open it. The opposition, momentarily caught off guard, countered by pointing out that nobody could be expected to call and say, "I can't attend the event, so don't open my bottle." The obligation not to open it remained.

While we were embroiled in this minor ethical dissertation, I was tasting a fair amount of 1940, 1952 and 1959 Château Latour. I noticed in time a certain weakening of resolve, a certain appreciation of the moment, and even a flush of generosity toward the donor who wasn't there.

And in this spirit of benevolence and diversion, when the future seemed an abstraction and the present so divine, I somehow lost my grip on the argument and the chairman prevailed. The 1899 Latour remained bottled-up, along with my reputation—I fear forever and ever.

WHICH WINE WITH ROAST DUCKLING?

This is called THE WINE COMPUTER MATING GAME, and it is not unlike the services that arrange dates between compatible people. The people send in their personality profiles and the computer pairs them, although I understand there are a few subscribers who would like to get their hands on the programmer.

We mate wine and food in similar manner. Every dish has a personality as does every wine. Here's the game: I describe the personality of the dish and offer three choices of wine. You arrange the date. The wine and the food report to me afterwards, and I grade your selection.

No, this has nothing to do with wine snobbery. Forget about that for a moment. This is educational. You can't be a wine snob unless you understand the basics. In wine, as in literature, you must study the classics.

The dish: poached striped bass

The wine: Chablis
            Muscadet
            California Chardonnay

The Analysis
A poached striped bass has a fragile, delicate

personality. The flavor is subtle and elusive, and it will not stand up to a confrontation. A Muscadet is appropriately nonaggressive but it's a little too fruity. Even *that* much assertion will intimidate a poached fish. A California Chardonnay, especially an oaky vinification, will overpower the dish altogether. The choice is Chablis, with its refined, austere, flinty character, like a Presbyterian minister.

The dish: sole amandine

The wine: Chablis
              Muscadet
              California Chardonnay

The Analysis

This is no longer exactly "fish," the toasted almonds having captured almost all the flavor. There is assertion here, and body to balance a wine. The Chablis, although acceptable, is too austere. The Chardonnay, although acceptable, is too combative. The Muscadet has the right combination of fruit and definition to complement the semisweet, nutty flavor of the sole.

The dish: striped bass livornese (with onions, black olives and mushrooms, in a spicy tomato sauce)

The wine: Chablis
              Muscadet
              California Chardonnay

The Analysis

Add an extra point if you answered, "None of the above." The best wine for a livornese preparation is a light red like Bardolino, Beaujolais or Spanish Rioja. This is a dish redolent with Mediterranean aromas. It really needs the fruit of the red grape.

Of the three choices, Chardonnay is best. The equation is simple: strong dish—strong wine. A Muscadet isn't bad, although it doesn't have the muscle to stand up to a spicy tomato sauce. A Chablis would get lost.

Now, some diverse entrées that have always challenged the wine computer.

The dish: roast duckling à l'orange

The wine: Pouilly-Fuissé
            Beaujolais
            red Burgundy

The Analysis

There can be endless discussion about roast duckling. It would be difficult to find a wrong wine as long as the wine was not light. A Chablis, for example, is not a good choice because the duck, no matter how it is prepared, is a lusty dish. That eliminates Pouilly-Fuissé, a white Burgundy of the same general character as Chablis.

A Beaujolais has the fruit and the spice, but the personality of roast duckling is not spicy. It has a deep, mellow flavor—very strong—with hints of nutty sweetness, with or without the orange sauce. Essentially it is too strong a dish for Beaujolais. The first choice would be a red Burgundy; a Chambertin would be lovely. Don't skimp here; the duck will bury a thin Volnay.

The dish: sweetbreads (simple preparation)

The wine: Chianti
            red Bordeaux
            white Burgundy

The Analysis

If you guessed Chianti subtract three points and return to whisky sours. Chianti is an aggressive wine; sweetbreads are a shy dish. However, "shy" is not to suggest lacking in character. Sweetbreads have a strong underlying character, a backbone, an individuality. It's just that the personality doesn't charge right out and confront you. It's restrained; you must draw it out.

Sweetbreads require a wine that has a similar inner strength. A white Burgundy, in the class of Montrachet or Meursault, would be perfect.

Well then, why not a red Bordeaux? Surely a red Bordeaux has inner strength. Yes, but it also has the intensity and flavor of the red grape—enough to intimidate sweetbreads.

The dish: beef bourguignon

CAVIAR & CHAMPAGNE

BEEF BOURGUIGNON With ZIN-FANDEL

POACHED STRIPED BASS & CHABLIS

SWEET-BREADS + WHITE BURGUNDY

The wine: red Burgundy
            California Zinfandel
            red Bordeaux

The Analysis

Although the classic wine for beef bourguignon is a strong red Burgundy—La Tâche, Musigny, Chambertin—no points are subtracted for Bordeaux or Zinfandel. The argument for Burgundy is that the beef is simmered in Burgundy and one should mate the table wine with the cooking wine. Well, maybe so.

This is a powerful dish, and if you've chosen red Bordeaux choose a strong one. A beef stew married to a Cos d'Estournel 1970 could live together long and happily. A Zinfandel, the strongest of the California reds, would also slug it out with a beef stew, and what a lovely battle!

The dish: caviar

The wine: Chablis
            Champagne
            Soave

The Analysis

Here again there is general agreement: The classic marriage is caviar and Champagne. Their personalities are compatible—aristocratic, high-strung. This is really a marriage among royal families.

If the computer did not factor in royalty, a fine, elegant, Grand Cru Chablis would be delightful. Soave, a rather unpolished, scrappy Italian white, would be out of place and uncomfortable.

If you scored well in THE WINE COMPUTER MATING GAME you have a natural talent for determining compatibility and a sound understanding of wine and food. This might suggest a career in computer programming, hotel management, or as a maître d'.

It might also suggest that your dinner parties are the talk of Scarsdale. If you've not heard words to that effect, proceed to the next chapter, It's Not the Food, It's the Preparation.

IT'S
NOT THE FOOD,
IT'S THE
PREPARATION

Mary Elizabeth, worried all week about a dinner party she's planning for twelve, calls the wine shop in town and asks for suggestions.

"I'm serving veal," she says.

"I'd recommend a white; perhaps a California Chardonnay."

"Goes well with veal?"

"Perfect with veal."

The conversation repeats itself in thousands of homes all over America as hostesses try to match the wine to the food. But the recommendation is not correct; the hostess has failed to mention how the veal is being prepared. In fact she is considering adding a blanket of ham and Jarlsberg cheese. The preparation calls for a red.

Another hostess, equally perplexed by the mystique and confusion of marrying wine to food, calls *her* shop. "I'm serving veal," she says.

"I'd suggest a light red. A 1973 red Bordeaux would be very nice."

Again the hostess has failed to consider (and the wine shop has failed to ask) the preparation. She has in mind a veal piccata, lightly breaded, with a strong accent of lemon.

The red Bordeaux would be O.K. but a Chardonnay would be perfect.

Indeed, all over America, hostesses are offering the wrong information and wine shops are supplying the wrong wine. It's not the food, it's the preparation.

We have at last outgrown the axiom RED WINE WITH MEAT, WHITE WINE WITH FISH. We seem to understand now that veal, lamb and chicken—even beef and fish—can be served with a red or a white. But we don't seem to be entirely clear about *why* or *when*. A simple approach explains it: Match the wine to the preparation.

Pairing wine and food does not require a degree from the Culinary Institute. It's a matter of good sense. Ignore the axioms and consider the *character* of the dish: Is it light or heavy, shy or assertive? Light dishes are complemented by light wines, heavy dishes by heavy wines. It sounds almost distressingly simple—and it is.

Fish is generally a light food, but how are you *preparing* the fish? Are you poaching it with a bit of butter or are you baking it in a casserole with mushrooms, onions and tomato? In the first case you should serve a light wine and in the second, a medium wine. A fish casserole is not a heavy dish—beef stew and veal parmigiana are heavy dishes.

Now, having evaluated the dish, evaluate the wine. Chablis, Muscadet, Sancerre and Pouilly-Fuissé are among the light wines. California Cabernet and Zinfandel, Italian Barolo and French Châteauneuf-du-Pape are among the heavy wines. Medium wines include California Chardonnay, Beaujolais, red Burgundy and red Bordeaux.

Having made these simplistic designations I can hear outraged cries from the wine experts: "How can you describe a Chambertin (red Burgundy) as medium? It's a strong wine!"

Absolutely true. Red Bordeaux and Burgundy cross all over the wine spectrum depending on the quality and the year. But we are dealing here with an approach; we can't classify each château.

Fish is hardly ever "heavy," a possible exception being a lusty fish stew like cioppino. Beef is hardly ever "light," a debatable exception being carpaccio, thin slices of raw beef, often in a type of vinaigrette sauce. But veal, lamb and chicken, depending on the preparation, can be either.

Liver is usually heavy. Served breaded and smothered in onions, liver is a strong dish. Served thin-sliced and pink in the pan juices, it is medium.

Sweetbreads, gently braised in the manner of The Quilted Giraffe, are light or medium-light. Breaded and served in a rich chestnut sauce in the style of Mon Paris, they are heavy. A broiled chicken is light (or medium-light); a chicken breast in cream sauce on a bed of spinach is medium; chicken in red wine, coq au vin, is heavy.

Anyone can judge this; there are no experts. Your evaluation of coq au vin is as valid as anyone's.

So forget about *rules* for matching wine to food. There is nothing absolute and nothing mystical about it. Nowhere does there exist a ten commandments. Nobody knows any more than good sense would suggest. Match the wine to the preparation and have a good time.

WHICH WINE?— WHICH FOOD?

"Which dessert would you order with a Trocken-beerenauslese?"

The question was asked of Peter Sichel, the speaker at a grand tasting of German wines. A fascinating question, I thought, as I sipped this incredibly honeyed liquid—the bottle priced at $100. I considered the possibilities: A floating island? A deep, rich, intense chocolate cake? A coupe aux marrons?

Peter thought about it a moment. An urbane, polished speaker—an expert on the wines of Germany—it was clear that he took the question seriously and that he would not be hurried into an answer. Finally, I detected a bit of a smile as though . . . yes . . . it had come to him.

"Lemon mousse," he said.

Lemon mousse: It was perfect. The absolutely clear counterpoint to one of the world's greatest sweet wines.

A Trockenbeerenauslese is a German Rhine wine, worthy rival to Château d'Yquem. Its extraordinary sweetness is also achieved by leaving the berries on the vine until they are attacked by the prestigious noble rot. At my table we nodded to each other. The marriage of lemon mousse to a

Trockenbeerenauslese was ideal. The sharp-edged, almost shocking flavor of the lemon would cut against the intense sweetness of the wine. Peter is always right, I thought, filing away the answer to be resurrected at some grand dinner, when inevitably we would be trading stories of the perfect wine with the perfect food.

This is what serious wine people do: They speculate about which dessert one has with a Trockenbeerenauslese, which wine accompanies foie gras, which wine complements oysters Rockefeller. It is—what shall we call it?—a wine game; a game that requires knowledge, experience, imagination, style and just a shade of daring.

Such a game cannot escape the notice of the wine snob.

Indeed, a reputation might be built upon a brilliant observation such as lemon mousse and Trockenbeerenauslese. Not Peter Sichel's reputation, of course; I mean the rest of us: anxious to order the correct wine, describe it in the correct way, and be thought of as a distinguished—no, not distinguished; *Peter* is distinguished—a discerning member of the wine community.

And so the wine snob catalogs brilliant unions of wine and food, always remembering that the key word is brilliant. He disdains the ordinary; he reaches for the unique. If you asked the sommelier in a good French restaurant which is the perfect wine for a venison stew he would guide you to a Châteauneuf-du-Pape. The wine snob is not interested in guiding; he is interested in impressing. A routine combination is tiresome. He would suggest a California Zinfandel.

If the dish were oysters Rockefeller, the wine snob would again reach for the imaginative. If the classic recommendation were Montrachet or Meursault, the wine snob offers a Sancerre. Of course, he must be careful; we are considering a complex dish: oysters baked with spinach and cream. A Beaujolais might be a daring yet acceptable proposal, but a classic red Burgundy—a Musigny, a Chambertin—is not a wine for oysters Rockefeller. The tightrope between daring and foolish demands exceptional balance.

Confidence and assertion are the trump cards in the game of WHICH WINE?—WHICH FOOD? If you wish to propose a Beaujolais with oysters Rockefeller, be fearless, and if challenged don't retreat.

"Have you ever tried it?" you might ask.

Now, consider other dishes and other wines. Which wine would you order with rognon de veau à la moutarde? A Rhone Valley wine? Well yes, but there are other choices: A California Cabernet Sauvignon, an Italian Barolo. Each could be argued with confidence.

Which wine would you order with bouillabaisse? Well, consider the dish: It is assertive but not quite robust. It's spicy, but the spice does not overpower. Ordinarily you might order a red Bordeaux of medium strength, possibly a Spanish Rioja. But the suggestion of a strong, oaky California Chardonnay could hardly be disregarded.

In the game of WHICH WINE?—WHICH FOOD? the wine snob gathers his information, considers his possibilities, and joins the players. He will be judged by the intelligence of his choice, but even more by his flair and imagination. A bit of the outrageous never hurt the reputation of the wine snob.

THE NOBLE SOCIETIES OF WINE AND FOOD

Among the distinguished wine societies in America are La Chaîne des Rôtisseurs, Les Amis du Vin, Les Chevaliers du Tastevin, and The Wine and Food Society. Sooner or later the aspiring wine snob must join at least one of them. Given the choice I might suggest La Chaîne simply on the elegance of the name. When your friends call for a round of poker you can say, "I'd love to but there is a meeting tonight of the Chaîne des Rôtisseurs." Don't concern yourself if you can't pronounce it—nobody will know.

The argument against the Chaîne is its uniform. Chaîne members wear a bright-colored sash over their shoulders and across their chests, and—listen to this—your rank in the society determines the color of the sash. Now ordinarily the traditions of wine snobbery would demand such pageantry, but Chaîne members go too far. I was dining with friends recently at a Chinese restaurant, and in a separate room the Chaîne was having an event. I know a lot of Chaîne members, and anxious to impress my friends, I suggested that we leave our noodles in sesame-seed oil and discover what the Chaîne was eating.

I was soon greeted by Chaîne members and of

course they were in black tie, their handsome ceremonial sashes cutting across their chests. Maybe they pin medals on the sash; I don't remember. After a few introductions my friends and I returned to our table.

"That's the wine group you belong to?" asked my friend.

"You wear one of those uniforms to the wine and food tastings?" asked the other.

"To eat *egg rolls*?"

It was embarrassing; there's no denying it. I struggled to explain that I belonged to The Wine and Food Society and not to the Chaîne des Rôtisseurs, but it was not a time for minor distinctions. My friends—whom I have spent years trying to impress with my standing in the gourmet community—had come face to face with the gourmet community.

That's the argument against La Chaîne des Rôtisseurs.

The Chevaliers du Tastevin—properly the Confrèrie des Chevaliers du Tastevin—is a serious and distinguished society whose interest is confined to the wines of Burgundy. All events of the Tastevin are black tie, and they also drape a crimson-and-gold ribbon over their shoulders, attached to the end of which is a tastevin, a dimpled silver cup traditionally used by professionals to taste wine.

The argument against Les Chevaliers du Tastevin is the length of the name. It's impossible to hold the attention of an indifferent audience when an otherwise fast-moving wine story is constantly interrupted with references to La Confrèrie des Chevaliers du Tastevin. This apparent oversight by the founders has not limited interest in the society. There is a waiting list.

The argument against Les Amis du Vin is that there is *no* waiting list. You send in twenty dollars—you become a member. You can also have it billed to MasterCharge, and I don't think we need dwell on a society whose membership fee is paid for like a pair of pajamas. It may be democratic, and democracy has its place, but not in the halls of wine snobbery.

The Wine and Food Society does not have a name

to match the Chaîne but they do have an event called the BYOB. You don't know what BYOB stands for? It stands for Bring Your Own Bottle, one of the great snobbery spectacles of all time. In order to be invited to the BYOB you must bring your own bottle, obviously. Of course, not any bottle will do. You can't suggest, as an offering to the gods, a thirty-pound bottle of, say, Château Talbot 1961. That won't even get you a seat in the bleachers. To attend the Bring Your Own Bottle event of The Wine and Food Society, you must part with something your grandfather left you.

Certainly that has wine snobbery written all over it. You mention to friends that you are attending a Bring Your Own Bottle event, and they naturally will be curious about which heirloom you are bringing.

"I'll probably bring a '45 Lafite."

There—you've done it. In six short words you have established yourself in the hierarchy of wine snobbery. Everybody knows how much Lafite costs.

Another event of The Wine and Food Society, and of the Chaîne des Rôtisseurs, guaranteed to dazzle your friends and admirers, is the vertical tasting. Your friend calls:

"There's a new Woody Allen movie at the Century. How about it?"

You pause a moment, just slightly disconcerting him. Just slightly suggesting that he might have, on occasion, a more challenging evening in mind.

"I might consider it, but the Chaîne des Rôtisseurs is having a vertical tasting of Château Pétrus tonight."

Your friend is bewildered. In a single sentence you have bombarded him with the Chaîne, Château Pétrus and the concept of a vertical tasting—three icons in the religion of wine snobbery.

Off-balance, he asks what a vertical tasting is, not aware that it will cost him fifteen minutes of oenological pontification, not to speak of an insufferable putdown.

"A vertical tasting," you respond, "occurs when

we taste a single wine over a span of years. In such manner we can judge the 1966 Pétrus against the 1964. We can also determine whether the 1953 vintage is fading and whether the 1970 vintage is ready to drink. It's essential to having a complete understanding of Château Pétrus or any other wine."

Nice work. You managed that with finesse and elegance. You did not offer the information; you were asked. Nor was it necessary to exhaust your palette of descriptive phraseology. You just told it the way it was.

Your friend is suitably impressed (and also without a companion for the movies). He tries someone else, and cannot help but mention that he called you also. "Do you know where Leonard is going tonight? To a meeting of the Chaîne des Rôtisseurs, for a vertical wine tasting."

"A *what?*"

On such foundation stones rests your reputation as a wine snob.

The Chaîne and The Wine and Food Society permit guests, not to fulfill social obligations, but rather to introduce potential members and serious wine people to the society's events. Nobody pays any attention to that, of course. You bring someone you're anxious to impress.

It's an important reason why a wine snob in training should try to join either society. Certainly there's someone in town—someone fashionable, sophisticated, imperious, arrogant—whom you are dying to impress the hell out of. It goes a long way to invite him to a vertical tasting of Pétrus, or to a Cabernet Sauvignon tasting of Mondavi, especially when you can mention in passing that Bob Mondavi is flying in to comment on the event.

If you are attempting to join either society but not yet succeeding, and if you get *invited* to a wine tasting, there are certain suggestions which, if carefully followed, could save you from ruining your reputation as an emerging wine snob.

1. *Don't volunteer anything.* You will be sitting at a table with eight or ten members and guests, and various wines will be tasted. The temptation will be to offer an extremely clever or knowledgeable comment. This is a minefield best circumvented. You *might* manage a comment with just the correct nuance, but the odds are against it. If asked whether you think the Cabernet is ready to drink, quickly turn to your host and say, "What do *you* think, Roger?"

2. *Don't act as though you just arrived from Omaha.* There is a temptation, in these exalted surroundings, to act kind of dumb. That's a conceit of another kind. It is not unlike the young lady taken to her first baseball game who asks, "Why are they wearing those cute little metal caps?"

You're there because you've expressed some interest in wine. If you start asking questions like "What's Cabernet Sauvignon?" you're there for the last time.

3. *Don't be a smart-ass.* If someone asks, "Do you think the Chardonnay has too much oak?" he means it. Don't answer, "I don't know—I drink mostly Riunite."

If the talk at the table seems terribly snobbish, remember that this is the major leagues of wine snobbery. If you don't like the dialogue, why are you trying to get into the society?

PART III

A young couple having dinner at
Lutèce ordered an 1890 Château Lafite-
Rothschild—price $1,200. André Soltner, the
proprietor, cautioned against such
an old wine, and suggested instead a
1961 Lafite, which was $400.

"We'll have one of each," the young man
responded, "so we can compare."

AT
THE CHATEAU

At a cocktail party in Larchmont recently we were standing around acting debonair. Reginald was part of the group, which means I don't have to mention what we were discussing. It may be automatically assumed that if wine is not being discussed Reginald goes down to the den to watch television.

Actually I don't know why Reginald gets invited to all these parties. His cadaverous appearance and single-minded area of concentration would seem to make him less than the Henry Kissinger of the cocktail party circuit. Nevertheless, he is always there, perhaps because hostesses think that wine talk is sophisticated. If you begin with that assumption, there is no denying that you can't throw a party without Reginald.

Everyone including me, of course, was sounding extremely snobbish and dropping statements like "When I visited Yquem last year . . ." or "When Gael and I had dinner at La Grenouille . . ."

The conversation drifted to the wines of the Rhone Valley, and someone mentioned the interesting fact that some of these robust, muscular red wines are made from about 10 percent white grapes. This surprised everyone in the circle, although naturally nobody let on—such an admission being the end of invitations and the beginning of an intimate relationship with the late show. Reginald listened quietly to the white grapes story and then said, "Yes, that's what they tell me at the château."

All eyes turned to Reginald. At the château? What château?

Now clearly he didn't mean any old château; he said *the* château. Did Reginald own a château? Nobody asked. It's not a question you ask. If America's most distinguished wine snob says *the* château you're expected to know which château he means.

"That's what they tell me at the château." It was perfect. And it does explain why Reginald is invited to all these parties while Kissinger is home having scrambled eggs.

Finally someone, a great deal more secure than I, asked Reginald which château, and Reginald mentioned that he was part of an investment consortium—only Reginald would use a word like consortium—that had purchased this château in the Rhone Valley. The question gave Reginald a platform from which to expound, which he did for about twenty minutes, mentioning also that a particular attorney in Manhattan was the group representative.

The following Monday morning the attorney received nine phone calls from "friends of Reginald" who wondered whether there were additional shares available.

The attorney immediately offered that the original investors had not realized a profit in seven years. He added that the château was difficult to manage and difficult to control from an investment standpoint, the investors relying on a French manager who was really beyond their supervision. All in all, the attorney painted a rather dismal financial picture, after which not one of the nine withdrew his offer.

"I think they just wanted to own part of a château," the attorney told me afterwards.

I thought his reply suggested an innocence not usually associated with Manhattan attorneys, especially after you receive their bills.

Of course they wanted to own a château, I thought. You want to be a wine snob? What better way than to go around talking about what's happening at the château?

Is it possible to own a château? Of course it's possible. As the art collector can buy a Renoir—albeit at some sacrifice—the wine snob can invest in a château. It takes some money, although the Rhone Valley investment was only fifteen hundred pounds a share, a good deal less than any Renoir.

Naturally, you want to pay some attention to which château. I don't think you have to—like Douglas Dillon—buy into Château Haut-Brion, but there are some names that will surely be met with a reaction less than enthusiastic. As there are Renoirs and Renoirs, there are châteaux and châteaux.

Nor must you necessarily purchase a château in France. Certainly it's the most snobbish possibility, but today the wineries in California are perfectly acceptable. Try to choose one with an elegant name like David Bruce or Clos du Val. One of the problems of owning part of a California winery is the name. You don't want to have to mention that you own a share of Gallo or Schramsberg.

Indeed, it is even possible to consider an investment in the Rhine or Moselle, but here it is *urgent* to consider the name. Mentioning at a cocktail party that you own a piece of Schloss Vollrads will clear the room.

My best advice is: Stick to France and invest as little as possible. This is not an exercise in financial strategy. It might, in fact, *cost* you some money. Wine snobbery can be an expensive pursuit.

But next to membership in the Chaîne des Rôtisseurs or The Wine and Food Society, owning a château is the surest measure of your standing in the wine community. Every six months there will be a meeting of the partners, so when friends ask you to dinner that night, you can say, "We'd love to, but there's a meeting of the château owners."

If *nobody* asks you to dinner that night I'm certain you'll find a way to mention it somehow.

THE WINE CELLAR: TO HAVE OR HAVE NOT

To have or have not. Actually that is not the question. The question is: What to *say* if you have not?

Of course it's better to have. You can keep a cellar book, paste in labels, buy a tastevin, and decant by candlelight. You can discuss authoritatively which wines "throw a sediment" and which cases you are "laying down," this being the everyday idiom of the cellar.

To have not means you can't discuss anything. You are cut off from the very language of wine snobbery.

If you do not have a cellar, you would hardly want to explain that you don't have room, or worse, that you don't have the money. While ostentation is not respected, a certain appearance of financial credibility is desirable.

You need a reason and the reason exists. When asked, with some show of impatience, why you do not have a cellar, you say:

"The thermostat."

That's all you say.

The questioner will nod in agreement and sympathy.

You see, the wine snob has a natural enemy. He lies awake at night trying to outwit him but nothing works. Nor is the enemy some grand and noble antagonist. Oh no—the wine snob is plagued by a tiny mechanical device, neither sophisticated nor expensive: the thermostat.

It's not difficult to explain. The reputation of the wine snob is controlled by his cellar, and his cellar is controlled by the thermostat. There appears to be a natural antagonism between thermostats and wine cellars—the thermostat's attitude being: I can't drink the wine so why should I protect it for someone else?

A wine cellar must maintain a reasonably even temperature, and in particular must avoid dramatic dips and rises. If your cooling system becomes petulant during the summer and refuses to function on a ninety-degree day, it can wipe out your entire collection. Similarly, if your heating system decides, "Why should I strain myself at zero when the cooling system refuses to work at ninety?" your cellar is a casualty loss.

And remember, this temperature control is necessary 365 days a year, twenty-four hours a day. If there's a power failure, if there's a malfunction while you are away on vacation, you can ruin a lot of wine. Because while the human body has learned to survive zero and ninety degrees, that is not quite good enough for a case of Bâtard-Montrachet. And while most of the precious things in this world— fine paintings, sculpture, diamonds, furs—survive vagaries of temperature, it will not do for Cheval-Blanc. Which is the reason why every wine snob respects *the thermostat*.

In any discussion about wine cellars, even those cellars with temperature-controlled units, you will observe much fretting over mechanical dependency. So the explanation "The thermostat" requires not another word.

If you don't care to use that excuse but still care about your reputation as a wine snob, your second choice is to buy a home in Chappaqua with a real stone cellar, set deep underground. I hear some are still available for under £125,000, and if you have anything left over you can lay down a case or two of Bardolino.

Almost any wine book will instruct you how to proceed. Almost every book has a chapter on building and stocking a cellar, and many books will offer a choice: a beginner's cellar, an expert's cellar, a poor man's cellar, a rich man's cellar. I believe, however, that the wine writers of the world have neglected the most important cellar of all, because I find no recommendations for a wine snob's cellar, universally regarded as the primary reason for bothering with a cellar at all.

The difference between a wine lover's cellar and a wine snob's cellar is this: A wine lover will lay down bottles that he enjoys drinking; a wine snob will lay down bottles he enjoys talking about. Certainly it's possible to do both. A case of 1966 Latour will protect you in either company. But a case of '66 Latour, while highly respected, is not the highest aspiration of the wine snob. It's simply too easy—a function of money rather than ingenuity. The true wine snob—as interested in discussing wine as drinking it—might search for Latour in an off year. And while everyone is talking about his 1966 Latour, you can quietly, but assertively, mention your case of '67.

"Yes," you acknowledge, "the '66 Latour is a lovely bottle if you care to part with £75, but have you tried the '67?"

(Well of course he hasn't tried the '67. People who can afford 1966 Latour don't bother with lesser vintages.)

"Is it nice?" he asks defensively, having lost control of center stage.

"Remarkable," you respond, aware that "remarkable" can mean many things.

In a word, the wine snob seeks the esoteric. Certainly he does not ignore the Grands Crus, but they are not provocative phrases in the language of the cellar. Everyone knows that '61 Lafite is great wine as everyone knows that Babe Ruth hit sixty home runs. You would hardly hold center stage in a baseball conversation with a moldy observation like that. The wine snob strains to suggest that while everyone with money can buy Lafite '61 (with lots of money, actually) it requires expertise to know about '67 Latour.

Expertise can be demonstrated by laying down a great wine in an off year, or a lesser wine in a great year. It can be demonstrated by knowing which vintner in Clos de Vougeot bottles the best wine, or which Cabernet Sauvignon bottled by Joseph Heitz is the most promising. It can be furthered by laying down a case of some extraordinary Italian Barolo or Gattinara, or a Spanish Rioja of exceptional quality or—who knows?—a wine from Lebanon or Australia. Expertise has always commanded more respect than money, which is why the ranks of snobbery are well represented by scholars of all types, and college professors in particular.

In the absence of expertise don't despair; there is still money. I remember a table I once sat around that included some enthusiastic and knowledgeable motorcar snobs. The dialogue went fast and furious with Peugeots and Jaguars and Mercedes flying back and forth, and much fuss being made over XKEs and 505s and who-knows-what. There was this quiet little guy at the table, listening intently and contributing nothing, when finally one of the XKEs turned to him—a bit exasperated, I thought—and asked what he drove.

"A Rolls," he said.

Yes, there is still money. A bit coarse, a bit vulgar, and certainly looked upon with disdain by the academic community, it can, nevertheless, be traded for a case of Romanée-Conti, the crown jewel of Burgundy. I assure you that a case of Romanée-Conti will stand up in any company. The experts will buzz around you with their '67 Latours, having researched their purchase down to the September rainfall levels and the cycles of fermentation. And you are well advised to avoid the banter, the fencing, the one-upmanship, and sit quietly until the betting and raising is over and the hands are shown. Like a Rolls, nothing beats a case of Romanée-Conti.

ESOTERICA

"On Monday we had lunch in Roanne; on Tuesday, dinner in Mionnay. On Wednesday we drove south to Madame Point's, where we had a marvelous poularde de Bresse. By the weekend we were dining in Crissier."

The above is a quote from one of America's most distinguished wine snobs. Read it carefully and then name the four restaurants referred to. You can't name all four? You can only name two? Well, O.K., but don't go around announcing it.

Is this a quiz? No, it is not a quiz. It is simply Reginald reciting his visits to the Continent's three-star restaurants. Reginald regards it as crass to mention a restaurant *name*. Why he does is not entirely appreciated by his understudies, which is probably why we are the understudies.

In a moment of incredible abandon, I once asked Reginald why he doesn't refer to La Pyramide as La Pyramide, instead of Madame Point's. He peered down from his throne and said, "One is expected to know which kitchen Madame Point presides over."

If you ever are thrust into a conversation with Reginald you must understand the language. When returning from a trip to Europe, one never mentions the name of a restaurant—one refers to the chef.

Where the chef and the restaurant are the same, such as Girardet's in Crissier, Switzerland, or Troisgros in Roanne, France, one refers to the town.

You have figured out by now—or at least I hope you have figured out by now—that the game is called Esoterica: a language developed to be understood by the chosen few. That's the way Reginald keeps the riffraff out of his life.

I want to be fair about this: The rules of the game are not inflexible. I have heard some reasonably polished wine and food snobs occasionally refer to Girardet's as Girardet's, to Troisgros as Troisgros. I have not, however, heard anyone refer to Troisgros and then proceed to explain that it is a three-star restaurant in Roanne. Or at least I have not heard it from anyone I would care to be introduced to.

And yes, there are exceptions. Paul Bocuse's restaurant outside of Lyon is often referred to as Bocuse (not Bocuse's—the wine snob is expected to have a feeling for the melody of the language). More appropriately one will mention that he had lunch in Lyon, and while Bocuse is not the only excellent restaurant in Lyon, he will be understood. Should that confuse you, the explanation is this: If you had lunch at any *other* Lyon restaurant you would mention the name. "Lunch in Lyon" can only mean one thing.

Another three-star exception is Paul Haeberlin's restaurant, the Auberge de l'Ill, in the town of Illhaeusern. It is not called Haeberlin's, possibly because Haeberlin is not quite as well known as Girardet or Troisgros, and it is not called Illhaeusern because nobody knows how to pronounce Illhaeusern. I'm afraid that only leaves Auberge de l'Ill, and that's what it's called. Reginald advises that he has never been there and will continue to avoid a restaurant that he must refer to by its name.

The final exception is Paris: It is not obligatory to refer to a Paris restaurant by the name of the chef. It is permissible to say you had lunch at L'Archestrate and not mention the name of Alain Senderens. It is *permissible*, mind you; no points are *lost* by mentioning Senderens, about whom it has been written, "Senderens's cuisine, subtle and delicate, can match Guérard's or even that of Freddy Girardet— today perhaps the world's leading chef."

Guérard's? Don't slip up on that one. The reference is to Michel Guérard, whose restaurant in Eugénie-les-Bains is world-famous. The name of the restaurant? Why nobody remembers the name of the restaurant. It would be a terrible indiscretion to refer to it by anything other than Guérard's. And should you feel that this exercise in snobbery is all fanciful and nothing more than whimsy, here's proof: I challenge you to ask any gourmet the full name of the restaurant in Eugénie-les-Bains. If he knows it at all he will answer, "Guérard's," in a manner to suggest that there is nothing more to say. If you persist, risking good sense and common courtesy, I am prepared to wager that the person *will not know* the name of Guérard's restaurant.

Those are the rules in the game of Esoterica, a game so selective and elusive that the wine snobs are not even aware that they are playing it. Much of Esoterica is played that way: The art experts say "Piero," when referring to Piero della Francesca. Jazz buffs speak of "Louis." It seems to be the best way to keep the right people in and the wrong people out.

LE TOUR GASTRONO- MIQUE

It is essential to refer to Troisgros and Bocuse with the correct shadings of arrogance and ennui, but you can't get away with that without a visit. The wine snob can command center stage, dropping "Chambertins" here and "Musignys" there, but wine leads to food, and suddenly someone mentions a bottle he ordered at Bocuse.

Bocuse! A magic word. The interest shifts. A new actor, suave and debonair, appears onstage. It is said in the theatre that a child will always steal the scene from a star, and in the kingdom of snobbery Paul Bocuse will always steal the scene from a Chambertin.

And Bocuse is inevitable. Any discussion on wine suggests a reference to food, and where there is food there is Bocuse. So if you are being upstaged regularly by Europe's three-star restaurants it might be time to consider Le Tour Gastronomique.

Sooner or later it must happen: You will be sitting at La Tulipe in New York enjoying a splendid preparation of chicken roasted with whole garlic cloves, and you will be speculating grandly on which wine complements the dish, when someone asks whether you've tried the version at Alain Chapel in Mionnay. (More likely, just Mionnay;

you're expected to know who's there.) Alain Chapel—the very sound of it intimidates. The very poetry of the language suggests intrigue and splendor. There is no adequate response. The great châteaux of the world will not save you.

You are at Dodin-Bouffant, on Fifty-eighth Street, trying their highly imaginative cuisine. "But have you tried the cassolette of truffles with asparagus at Girardet? The aiguillettes de canard at Troisgros? The petite bouillabaisse at La Mère Blanc?"

Finally there is nothing left to do but to plan Le Tour Gastronomique: eight three-star restaurants in eight days. The very best of the world in a single urgent ten-day trip.

It can be done. Perhaps it cannot be done leisurely or gracefully, and surely there is no argument against twenty-one days. But perhaps you would prefer China or Israel for twenty-one days (no Tour Gastronomique there) and accomplish the three-star adventure in a week. After all, we are not arranging a vacation, but protecting our reputations as wine snobs.

It requires planning, money, caution and dispatch. There is no room for miscalculation: All reservations must be confirmed. There is no room for gastric disorder: An upset stomach ruins the trip. But it can be done, and never again will someone steal center stage with "Bocuse."

"Bocuse? Yes, it's quite nice, but don't you agree that it's too much pageantry? Don't you think they are more serious in Roanne?"

The Tour Gastronomique begins with a study of geography: Where can you find eight three-star restaurants in the same vicinity? Paris? Well, you can find six, but it will not do. It is generally agreed that France's greatest restaurants today are outside of Paris. The old hierarchy of Lasserre, Tour d'Argent and Taillevent has some weak links. A map leads you unquestionably to Lyon, where the great triumvirate of Bocuse, Chapel, Troisgros are all within a hour's drive. From that center you look outward. Chez la Mère Blanc is an hour to the north. Girardet and Père Bise are two hours to the east. Pyramide is less than an hour south. And finally there is still Paris.

What follows then, with some apologies, is a brief culinary travel guide. Eight restaurants—eight days. Your reputation ensured forever.

There are several approaches but they all include the center: Bocuse, Chapel and Troisgros. You can eliminate Girardet and Père Bise in favor of Pyramide in Vienne and Albert Pic in Valence. But Girardet's kitchen is miraculous and it permits you to spend a day in Geneva. Once Girardet is included the maps suggest Père Bise, which might be the loveliest three-star inn in France and offers your trip some balance and sanity. Another approach is to include Lameloise, in Chagny, considerably extending the boundaries to the north. Anything is possible but here's an itinerary you will not regret.

Begin at Girardet, flying directly to Geneva—landing early Saturday morning—and driving to Crissier for lunch, an hour easily from Geneva. You will have no difficulty understanding why many consider it the best restaurant in Europe. Order their Menu de Dégustation, or whichever multi-course menu the waiter recommends. Relax; you are in the hands of a master.

Remain overnight in Geneva and leave on Sunday for France and L'Auberge du Père Bise in Talloires, about an hour south of Geneva. Dinner at Père Bise Sunday night. Enjoy the setting—breathtaking. Worth the trip even without the three-star cuisine. Again (and always) order the grand menu—in this case 320 francs or about £30 a person without wine or apéritifs (but including service). Overnight Sunday at Père Bise.

At each of these restaurants dinner is staged differently than at home. You will be offered a special apéritif—often Champagne, with crushed raspberries or eau de framboise (you would not want to ask for a Martini)—and with the apéritif will be served a small tray of hors d'oeuvre, specialties of the chef: At La Mère Blanc, a tiny cassolette d'escargots with mushrooms; at Troisgros, coeurs de canard, sautéed in butter with fines herbes.

Dinner will proceed through a variety of courses, generally five or six if you order the grand menu, and then a cheese board will be suggested offering twenty or thirty cheeses.

Then dessert. At home this means a single dessert: strawberry shortcake or coupe aux marrons. In France it means a dessert cart, decorated with a galaxy of pastries, fruits and sherbets. You may try whatever you like. At Girardet you might begin this extravaganza with assorted sherbets, a small scoop of each of five: grapefruit, lime, tea (yes!), pineapple and rhubarb. Then on to pastries, probably a thin slice of three or four, and nobody will mind if you would finally like to sample their floating island. Coffee follows, along with a tray of petits-fours and chocolates. This is three-star dining in Europe.

Monday: a two-hour drive to Lyon. Lunch or dinner at Bocuse; overnight in Lyon. Tuesday: an hour's drive west to Roanne. Dinner and overnight at Troisgros. Wednesday: one and one-half hours to Mionnay. Dinner and overnight at Alain Chapel. Arrive on time and leave early. Dinner is the attraction; the town of Mionnay is almost nonexistent.

Thursday: an hour's drive north to Vonnas and Chez la Mère Blanc, where Georges Blanc's kitchen compares to anything in France. Lesser known than Bocuse and Troisgros, it is nevertheless an absolute must on Le Tour Gastronomique.

Finally, I think, north to Paris—a four-hour trip but worth it for Friday's dinner at L'Archestrate, the temple of nouvelle cuisine, and Saturday's at Taillevent, year after year the standard against which classic cuisine must be measured.

Sunday: Air France to New York—armed with Paris, Lyon, Roanne, Mionnay—and, indeed, having experienced the wit, imagination and skills gastronomique of the world's great kitchens.

THE SZECHUAN
SOLUTION

On the Tour Gastronomique you can control the reservations and the expense, but there is a serious problem that you cannot control: The human body is not constructed to absorb eight 3-star dinners in eight days. The digestive system is assaulted with foie gras, mousseline sauce, custard pastries—and the bacteria of a foreign soil. Within three days it revolts. The first sign is a feeling of fullness accompanied by the mildest suggestion of nausea. You walk quickly past the pâtisserie windows. The cheese shops, suddenly, are no longer interesting. It is the brain announcing to the digestive tract that one more cream sauce and the system will black out.

Too bad, because tonight you had scheduled Troisgros, and the mere thought of Troisgros—even allowing for today's nouvelle cuisine—triggers an alarm system in the body. The stomach warns the brain that it will not contemplate three stars, and the brain sounds the alarm. It's all over for the Tour Gastronomique.

This is a major problem and it must be anticipated. There is virtually no question that eight 3-star restaurants in eight days will result in gastric insurgency. There are, however, solutions. They are practical and they are serious, and although they may not meet with uniform agreement from the gastroenterologists they will save your trip. You have two choices: to please your doctor or to preserve your reputation. No wine snob will have trouble with that decision.

There are four recommendations because there are many digestive systems. Some respond to certain treatments, some to others. Probably the most uniformly reliable approach—and the simplest—is mineral water *with* gas. It seems to create some kind of chemical scouring action in your stomach, neutralizing the butter and cream.

Keep the mineral water in your car and in your room, and be sure it's accessible during the night. Sip it regularly whether you're thirsty or not and begin at the beginning of the trip. Don't wait until the green monster starts creeping up on you. Different brands have different characteristics and Perrier doesn't work for me. Possibly it's me, but I would suggest another brand.

The second recommendation is yogurt. Apparently the yogurt cultures are natural enemies of foie gras cultures, and attack on sight. If this explanation exceeds all scientific reason, remember this is not a biology course. This is how to eat more incredibly rich food in a shorter time span than the body can possibly endure. Yogurt works, and there's nothing wrong with having some even before your first dinner, thus allowing the red army to deploy before the blue army attacks.

Next is the apéritif Fernet-Branca, some of the bitterest-tasting stuff in the world. Fernet-Branca is not a precautionary measure; you order it after the green monster gets a foothold and threatens your dinner that night at Troisgros. You order it in the late afternoon from any bar, and what it seems to do is paralyze the stomach: an alimentary novocaine shot. The nausea is cauterized; the appetite returns, and dinner at Troisgros is saved.

Fernet-Branca is a curious liqueur. It is described on the label as "a bitter stimulant to the appetite." Its magical powers might be explained by its exotic ingredients: aloes, gentian, zedoary, cinchona, calumba, galangal, rhubarb, bryonia, angelica—there's more—myrrh, chamomile, saffron and peppermint oil. Or in other words, a medicinal for whatever's wrong with you.

When you taste it for the first time—or even the second time—you may wonder whether Troisgros is worth it. Fernet-Branca is potent stuff. The sting may be eased, however, by a few drops of crème de menthe. The impact is not compromised, and an hour later you will begin to observe the signs of gradual recovery. On to Roanne!

Finally there is the Szechuan solution, a pleasant, practical, understandable approach to gastric disorder. Remember, of course, that gastric disorder—as defined here—is too-much-foie-gras, evidenced by a creeping fullness. It is not sharp pains or vomiting. The Szechuan solution is simply this: You've had too much cream sauce? It's time for an egg roll. It's time for a Chinese restaurant. So one day for lunch instead of a slice of pâté, a wedge of Camembert, and a strawberry tart, get a bowl of hot and sour soup. You have no idea what hot and sour soup will do to a cream sauce accumulation. It clears your pipes like Drano.

I'm absolutely serious. Perhaps it's the vinegar; perhaps it's the spices; but hot and sour soup (and Chinese food in general) neutralizes the cream and butter and fat, and leaves you feeling terrific. Now Chinese food doesn't mean a six-course banquet. That's what you're having tonight at Bocuse. Chinese food is a fix—a solution to the problem. Which doesn't mean that you can't enjoy it; you just can't stuff yourself with it.

Will you find a Chinese restaurant in the gourmet capitals of France? Yes you will, and you will be surprised at how many there are. But you have alternatives. What Chinese food does, Thai and Indian foods do. A curry sauce is wonderful. On to Bocuse!

LE SNOB GASTRONO- MIQUE

Snobbery is relative. Château Haut-Brion '66 is a lovely wine, but you can't drop it on a group that lays down '61 Lafite. A Picasso on the wall is impressive, but among those who collect Blue Period and Cubist, the wrong Picasso is worth a yawn.

So the Snob Gastronomique, who has just returned from a three-star culinary tour and wants to drop Bocuse and Troisgros at the Saturday night cocktail party, must consider the field he's dropping it on. Bocuse and Troisgros are impressive in most parts of town but there are travelers who have experienced almost all of the three-star restaurants of Europe. In such a crowd, Bocuse is Late Period Picasso, valuable but not classic.

If you find yourself in such company you will be aware of it at once. Travelers who have visited the world's three-star restaurants are not reticent about discussing their itinerary. One solution is escape; another is attack. But which restaurant do you attack with? Bocuse? Troisgros? Pyramide? I'm afraid not. In high-class gourmet society they are old hat. They have been around the longest; they are the best-known; they are central stops on the Lyon tour; and Bocuse, at least, is an international

celebrity. I need not emphasize that anything international and anything close to celebrity status does
not travel well in snob society.

Well then, what about Paris and its six 3-star
restaurants? Sadly, you can't mention Paris either.
Everyone has been to Paris (or at least everyone
who you would want to spend a few minutes talking
to) and everyone has a Paris story. If you get into
Paris restaurants it's a question of who shouts the
loudest. Worse, the Paris restaurants are no longer
thought to be the equal of the provinces. Taillevent
and l'Archestrate still rate a nod in snobbery circles,
but Lasserre and Vivarois will get you nothing more
than a cold stare of disbelief. Evidence: Mimi
Sheraton on Lasserre:

> . . . the pretentious and corny Lasserre, with its
> ceiling that slides open, its fried bread sculptures
> and backdrop of piano music, serves food that would
> be considered acceptable at a hotel-catered banquet.

That covers nine 3-star restaurants you cannot
mention. There are two more: Le Moulin de
Mougins and L'Oasis, near the southern coast of
France and along what might be described as the St.
Tropez–Cannes route. *Everyone* travels that route
(the Riviera beaches are not without their own
three-star attractions) and everyone has bumped
into Mougins and L'Oasis.

No. The restaurants that you drop in gourmet
stratosphere must combine a miraculous kitchen, a
remote location and a public-relations arm less
active than that of Paul Bocuse.

Among the best of these is Girardet, in Crissier,
Switzerland. Admittedly Crissier is within an hour
of Geneva, but Geneva is not along any gourmet
route. For every five visitors to Bocuse, only one
has tried Girardet. The kitchen is nothing less than
miraculous, and the restaurant—only in existence
for twelve years—has spent its time concentrating
on the menu and not the advertising. Look in any
bookshop window that promotes gourmet books:
twenty-seven by Bocuse, five or six by Troisgros, a
few *Michelin* guides, a *Kléber* and a *Gault-Millau*.
Nothing by Girardet. Now that's the stuff snobbery
is made of.

In the class of Girardet is Michel Guérard's restaurant in Eugénie-les-Bains. Four hundred fifty miles from Paris and in the middle of nowhere, you have to *aim* for Eugénie-les-Bains. A wondrous kitchen, a remote location and an underpaid advertising agency, Guérard is always spoken of with reverence. And yet, if you polled the gourmet

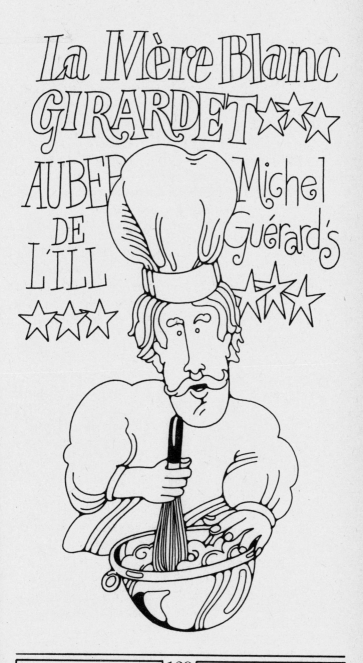

societies of America, Guérard, although well known, might be least visited. I think it's safe to say that someone who has dined at Guérard would not even bother to speak with someone who has dined at Bocuse.

Next might be Paul Haeberlin's restaurant, the Auberge de l'Ill in Illhaeusern. To describe Illhaeusern as merely remote would be to concede a presence that is undeserved; Illhaeusern is a blink of the eye. It is located in Alsace along a reasonably popular route, but its profile is even lower than that of Eugénie. You can safely drop Illhaeusern—best pronounced during a seizure of acute nasal congestion—in any crowd.

Chez la Mère Blanc, in Vonnas, is perfect because it just received its third star in *Michelin*. Naturally no Snob Gastronomique would be discovered dining in a two-star restaurant, and so La Mère Blanc was unheard of, except by a few culinary fanatics who seemed unaware that an interest in gourmet dining is always coupled with an interest in snobbery. Les Snobs Gastronomiques are racing to catch up, but novelty is still on your side. La Mère Blanc, a charming inn in a pleasant little country town, is about an hour from civilization. The kitchen is exceptional (and you needn't mention the swimming pool).

Remember always that Le Snob Gastronomique—like all snobs the world over—combines a delicate balance of timing, taste, pretension and understatement. You do not bother with Blue Period Picasso where simply Picasso will do. You do not mention Fauve Period Vlaminck to those unaware that Vlaminck painted with the Fauves. Similarly, it is both a waste of time and a miscalculation to drop La Mère Blanc where Bocuse is considered the shrine of gourmet dining. La Mère Blanc will sound like a feather falling.

If all of this seems tiresome you can forget the cause of snobbery. It is entirely possible to travel the Tour Gastronomique solely for the sake of food. My own view, however, is that it is an unwarranted extravagance, an unimaginative approach, a sign of an unbalanced personality, and a waste of time.

A
LESSON IN
BEAUJOLAIS

I knew that I was in the presence of a master when I
met Jean Beaudet at a Beaujolais tasting last year.
Jean is the director of the house of Paul Beaudet,
one of the distinguished wineries in the Beaujolais
area. Now normally Beaujolais is considered a
pleasant country wine and not high on the list of
wines around which you build a reputation for
snobbery—but all rules have exceptions.

There were eight of us around a table tasting the
wines of Beaujolais—tasting Fleurie, Morgon,
Juliénas and Moulin-à-Vent—and when the Morgon was poured it appeared to be a bad bottle. We
were all disappointed, and we asked Mr. Beaudet to
come to our table and taste the wine.

He lifted the glass, twirled the wine, brought it to
his nose—then waited a moment and put the glass
back on the table. Well, that took care of the sniffing
part, I thought; now he'll taste it. But the glass
remained where it was.

"The wine is good," he said. "Give it a few
minutes; it will come around." In a few minutes it
came around.

Consider: A table of eight fairly experienced wine
enthusiasts—some of us insufferable wine snobs—
had thought the wine bad enough to ask the lecturer

to taste it, and he didn't even taste it. He smelled it. That was enough for Jean Beaudet. It was also enough for me: I elected him at once to my personal Hall of Fame of Wine Snobbery.

We have discussed gestures that suggest some refinement in the world of wine snobbery. We have discussed sniffing and twirling, decanting and letting-the-wine-breathe. But there is no single gesture so polished, so aristocratic, so expert, as judging a wine without tasting it.

Nor is there a single gesture so risky. Because if you are sitting at dinner with another couple and you attempt this aerial somersault, be certain that your expertise matches your arrogance—there is no net. The wine will be poured, and if it doesn't match your pronouncement—if the wine is unsound—you had best be on the next train heading anywhere.

THE RAINS CAME

The world's most professional weather reports are heard on the eleven o'clock news, as you might expect, and at The Wine and Food Society, as you might not. Anyone interested in climatic conditions in France can find out—at any wine tasting in America—more information than he will care to know. And not only can he determine the *current* prevailing weather conditions, he can also discover the weather conditions during 1964 and 1970, should he be contemplating a trip in a time machine.

Virtually all wine enthusiasts are amateur meteorologists, their specialty being rainfall levels, and so a cult has built up around rainfall, bringing it inevitably to the attention of the wine snob. At any tasting of French wines you will hear, "The rains came late in 1964."

Don't think this is an announcement of merely passing interest. Rainfall is what makes the vines grow and the grapes ripen. If it falls in a disorderly pattern it can ruin a vintage.

I realize that sounds capricious, but consider this: If the rain falls in great buckets just before the vintners are planning to harvest and press, the grapes swell with water and the juice becomes thin.

So when you are tasting a particularly thin wine you will often hear the pronouncement "The rains came late." This is usually said at a wine tasting with an air of solemnity, otherwise reserved for natural catastrophes such as floods and earthquakes.

It requires a superb memory (or countless hours reading the rainfall charts) to remember whether the rains came late or early—or maybe not at all—in Burgundy during 1964. Still, you would be surprised how many wine snobs can do it. And in fact it is one of those exquisite jewels of information that distinguishes the wine snob.

You can be sitting around a table tasting a 1971 Pommard, and one person will claim it is ready to drink while another will claim it is not. A third might suggest it has too much tannin; a fourth could argue that the tannin is in perfect balance. A fifth can claim it has too much oak, meaning it has probably remained too long in the cask, or possibly that the oak was new. A sixth can claim that the oak is necessary to the structure of the wine. All valid positions, permitting discussion and disagreement. But if the wine is thin (and there is generally no debate about *that*) and if a person says, "Of course it's thin; the rains came too late in 1971," he is regarded at once as the leading wine snob and is deferred to.

There is even a rarefied strata of information that exceeds a degree in meteorology: a level so profound, so esoteric, and so intimidating that it clearly outranks rainfall patterns. Yes, it is expert to know that the rains came late during 1964, but which châteaux picked the grapes before the rains came? Two châteaux could lie side by side, and yet one owner might pick his grapes a week earlier than the other. During that crucial week the rains could come, entirely changing the character of the grape crop and consequently the wine.

To know that is to be armed with the most sophisticated weaponry in the combat zone of wine snobbery. While Snob A might suggest ordering a red Bordeaux, and Snob B might caution that "The rains came late," Snob C outclasses both of them by mentioning, "But not at Cheval-Blanc."

And *why* not at Cheval-Blanc? Well, listen carefully because this is really delicious, not to mention useful at your next dinner party. The rains did not come late at Cheval-Blanc because Cheval-Blanc is located in a district called St. Emilion and not in the Médoc district from which most red Bordeaux come. Are the rainfall patterns different in St. Emilion and the Médoc? Is that the reason? An intelligent guess, but wrong. It's the *grape patterns* that are different. In St. Emilion the dominant grape is the Merlot, while in the Médoc the dominant grape is the Cabernet Sauvignon. The Merlot matures earlier than the Cabernet Sauvignon and is therefore picked earlier. So it is entirely possible to harvest the Merlot in St. Emilion before the rains come, and harvest the Cabernet in the Médoc afterwards. And that is what happened during 1964, explaining why the St. Emilions and Pomerols, such as Cheval-Blanc and Pétrus, are wonderful, while the Médocs are just respectable. Drop *that* bit of information at your next wine tasting, why don't you?

Before you memorize the precipitation charts of a dozen wine countries and over a twenty-year period, let me make this job easy for you: You only have to do France. Italy and Spain, and California as well, seem to have even-tempered rainfall patterns and considerably less variable climatic conditions than France. Furthermore their wines are not quite as delicately balanced. When the rains come at Chambertin and Richebourg it is quite a different matter from when the rains come in Chianti. Nobody goes around saying, "The rains came late in Chianti."
So it is only France that you must learn, and even in France you can ignore the Loire Valley, Alsace, Champagne and the Beaujolais regions. It is not that the rain doesn't matter there, but it doesn't matter as much. That leaves Bordeaux, Burgundy and the Rhone Valley. Not bad: three regions multiplied by about twenty years, or sixty rainfall charts. Of course, if you intend to be serious about this, you will have to distinguish between the northern Bordeaux area, where the grapes of Lafite

and Latour grow, the southern Bordeaux area, where the grapes grow at Château d'Yquem, and even the middle Bordeaux, which includes Haut-Brion.

You can now understand why rainfall patterns are crucial to the wine snob, and also why analysis of the data is not just a routine matter. Perhaps, up till now, you've been wondering why you purchased this book, loaded as it is with information of less than the encyclopedic distinction. Now you know—to learn about Merlot and Cabernet, about St. Emilion and the Médoc, and about when the rains came. Accordingly you might wish to show your gratitude by passing out a few copies of this epic among your friends, thus ensuring that the writer has sufficient resources to keep a modest supply of St. Emilion maturing in his cellar.

OLD IS GOOD—NEW IS BAD

The cornerstones of snobbery have one consistent quality: *age*. Credentials are built upon old wealth, old rank and old family. Nothing "new"—nothing nouveau—has ever won respect.

A collector might own a Jackson Pollock—a lofty perch from which to look down upon his neighbor. But he would want to be certain that the living room he was looking down upon did not contain a Rembrandt. It has nothing to do with money; a Pollock could sell for as much as a Rembrandt. It has to do with age.

A person might drive a new custom-made Cadillac. It could have every convenience, every appointment. It might cost an incredible amount of money. But in the hierarchy of snobbery it would pale before a 1946 Packard.

Nor would a Steuben glass sculpture—one of a kind and signed—stand up to a Louis Tiffany lamp. Nor would anything turned out of the lathes and pinions of the Industrial Revolution stand up to Chippendale.

So it is with wine: Age, endurance and tradition count. The flashy new California wineries have style and pizzazz; but it is awfully difficult to be snobbish about a 1974 Mayacamas. Granted that the wine is wonderful and that the bottle is expensive. Trade it at once for a sleepy old 1960 Brane-Cantenac.

How about a 1976 La Tâche? Distinguished wine, exceptional vintage. Can you establish yourself in the wine community with a case of '76 La Tâche? Of course not—it is *contemporary*.

Recognizing these standards, the wine snob abjures any notion that might suggest youth. At best, youth is tolerated. Age is venerated.

Therefore—

"THE WINE IS NEVER READY"

You order a 1971 Musigny, an exceptional Burgundy in an exceptional year. The waiter pours a bit and you try it. It's quite lovely. Nevertheless, that is not your response. To concede that anything in this world not much older than a decade is *ready* is to misunderstand entirely the standards of snobbery. The indicated response is to sigh and to suggest, "What a pity to drink it now; it is only a child."

It would require a lengthy discourse to explain when the wine *might* be declared ready. In Bordeaux, a 1961 Lafite is still not ready twenty years later. A safe rule is this: If in doubt show compassion, and mention that one day the wine may be great. It is difficult to dispute, and it shows that you are accustomed to drinking wines that *are*.

Naturally we are talking about red wines. White wines get ready quickly and are consequently not as interesting as reds since you can't spend a few hours discussing whether they are ready or not. White wines are tasted mainly during the months of July and August anyway, when the rules of wine snobbery are adjourned.

"THEY DON'T MAKE WINES THE WAY THEY USED TO"

Well of course they don't make wines the way they used to. They don't make anything the way they used to. And incidentally, "they" is us.

But this is being pragmatic, and we are not dealing in matters of pragmatism, but in matters of snobbery. If you want to deal in pragmatism, join a debating group. Snobbery demands that you rail against the contemporary: Chambertin is no longer Chambertin; Lafite is no longer Lafite. The inescapable inference is that when Lafite *was* Lafite, some of the privileged can still remember the days when Daddy served it with the evening meal. Oh dear, those *were* the days, weren't they?

Finally we come to the classic confrontation of age and youth: the French Bordeaux against the California Cabernets. The French Bordeaux, centuries old; the California Cabernets, decades. Certainly we know where our allegiance lies. And yet, in tasting after tasting, the Cabernets are winning all the awards against the best wine Bordeaux has to offer. At the Ottawa tasting, in January 1981, California wines won the first five places, defeating Lafite, Latour, Margaux, Haut-Brion and Mouton. Unbelievable! The Bordeaux were all from the 1970 vintage, probably the best vintage since 1961. Imagine a 1970 Lafite losing to a 1974 Sterling Vineyards. What is the wine snob to say to that?

Perhaps it is wiser to consider what he cannot say. He cannot acknowledge—regardless of the evidence—that these California upstarts are the equal of wines that Napoleon drank. If questioned about the Ottawa tasting, he might simply ignore the question, or possibly regard the questioner with the kind of disbelief that would be the natural response had he been asked to compare Jackson Pollock to Rembrandt.

And it *is* true that the 1970 Bordeaux are probably a decade away from their prime, while the 1974 California Cabernets seem to be mature right now. "Try the comparison in 1990," you might say, secure that your challenge is unanswerable.

Avoid specifics and remember your stance: Old is good; new is bad. It will cost you an opportunity to order a delightful Mondavi Cabernet 1975, but it will ensure your reputation in the legions of wine snobbery. Be certain you are convinced of which is more important.

UNDER-STANDING OAK

Possibly you do not understand oak, and that's O.K. because oak is a perfectly boring subject. That does not, however, limit its discussion at wine tastings. A California Chardonnay will be poured and tasted, and someone at the table will comment, "Too much oak." A solemn nodding of the heads will follow as though nine justices of the Supreme Court had pronounced unanimously on a First Amendment violation. You might as well nod also; this is not the place to make your stand. Too-much-oak is simply a matter of opinion.

Boring or not, oak has worked its way into the language of wine snobbery along with soil contents and fermentation cycles. Certainly it has no stature. It cannot turn heads like a bottle decanted or convey expertise like a vintage chart remembered. It is one of those esoteric little subjects, neither grand nor fashionable, that fills the dictionary of wine snobbery.

Wine is aged in oak casks before bottling, and the oak becomes involved in the character of the wine. It imparts an astringency, which time tends to mellow, as well as a flavor, a balance and a "style." Many wine enthusiasts prefer an oak taste and many wineries develop that taste as part of the style of their wine. (Others will argue that they buy wine to taste the fruit and not the barrel.)

A winery that values a strong oak taste for style or balance can leave the wine in the casks longer than usual or can use new or scraped casks (scraping the inside of the cask cuts away the old residue and gets closer to the wood). There are also different oaks, French, German and American, and they each lend their own character.

Finally—and I don't want to dwell on this in a scholarly dissertation—not all the "oak" comes from the casks. Casks are expensive—to scrape or to buy—and winemaking is an industry that requires intensive capital. (Consider how long it takes, through growing, fermenting, aging, bottling and selling, to turn the grape juice into money.) It follows then that some winery would one day enjoy a bountiful harvest and not have the money for the casks. Use last year's casks? Yes, but last year's wine has absorbed the oak. Store the wine in stainless steel until oak becomes available? Yes, but wine is a "living thing"; you can't play around with its aging cycle.

Well, what then? You have the wine; you need the oak. What do you do? I don't want to say, but rumor has it that some wineries—only in a state of absolute desperation of course—have added oak "chips" to the aging wine. And I further understand that instead of *adding* the oak chips, it is possible to steam the oak chips and then condense the vapor into—I hesitate to mention it—liquid oak flavoring.

Before becoming too indignant perhaps we ought to consider components of other consumer products. Which product for instance contains monosodium glutamate, disodium inosinate and disodium guanylate?* I'll give you a hint: We take it when we're sick.

You can't blame industry for being inventive. The consumer demands and industry supplies—the cornerstone of the free marketplace. Possibly, here and there, demand and supply become irreconcilable, requiring some ingenuity and invention. Thus, liquid oak. It is not an issue to be debated, however, at the next comparative tasting of California Chardonnays.

*Chicken soup.

DEATH
OF THE WINE
SNOB

The taller the tree, the louder the crash. The grander the wine snob, the greater the delight when he stumbles.

That should surprise no one, nor should the discussion last month at Meredith's house when she served a Zinfandel with dinner to a group of serious wine and food people.

Picture the table: host and hostess at either end; three people on each side. The middle person on the far side is Hamilton, a renowned and infuriating wine snob. The Zinfandel is placed on the table— consider this carefully—with the label facing away from Hamilton. The wine is white.

"What are we having?" asks Hamilton, warming up to the moment when he will explain the wine in endless detail.

"A Zinfandel," shouts Meredith from the kitchen.

"Yes," says Hamilton, "but right now?"

"A Zinfandel," says Donald, who sits across the table from Hamilton and knows very little about wine but is twelve inches away from the label.

Donald's proximity doesn't appear to disturb Hamilton, who is blinded to everything but his own certainty. "If we're having Zinfandel," he declares, "bring it out and take away this bottle of white."

By this time everyone at the table is enjoying himself immensely, and wondering how deep Hamilton will bury himself. It's not that they are experts on Zinfandel, but they assume Meredith knows which bottle she placed on the table, and they assume Donald knows how to read.

Hamilton, who assumes nothing but his own importance, doesn't even turn the label but proceeds to explain that Zinfandel is not only red but a deep purple-red and probably the strongest red wine vinified in California.

Finally Donald turns the bottle so that the label faces Hamilton. The winery is Monteviña; the wine is white Zinfandel.

"Some kind of a joke?" Hamilton asks.

Call the play *Death of the Wine Snob.*

Consider Act II. We are at Gloria and Arthur's house for dinner, real people living in Larchmont, home of more than one wine snob. Neither Gloria nor Arthur is a wine snob, however, nor are they even aspiring wine snobs. This has annoyed me over the years, but not quite enough to break up the friendship.

Gloria and Arthur have a wine cellar; it came with the house. In the entire cellar they have possibly twenty bottles scattered around, and not the faintest idea of what any of them are. When Rita and I come for dinner they open a few bottles, always trying to open the best ones they have.

It's interesting to discover what Arthur has buried in his cellar because Arthur is a member in good standing in the financial community, and people are always giving him a few bottles when he merges their companies. Generally these bottles are appropriate to the occasion: One doesn't give a Beaujolais as a gift for a million-pound merger. Arthur doesn't know a Beaujolais from a Chambertin so he just throws them all together like bottles in a three-dollar wine bin sale. When we arrive Arthur shouts up from the cellar:

"Would you rather have a Beaujolais or—wait a second, I don't know how to pronounce this— CHAM-BER-TIN?"

"Which year Chambertin, Arthur?" (Not that it would matter.)

"1971."

"O.K., the Chambertin."

"What else should I bring up? We're having filet mignon. Oh, here's a bottle that might be O.K." He spells it out: "S-A-N-C-E-R-R-E. Is that any good?"

"It's terrific, Arthur, but it's white. I don't think we want a white wine with filet."

Silence for a moment . . . then, "Leonard, I think it's red."

"It's not red—what else do you have?"

"Leonard, come down here and take a look. It looks red to me."

"I don't have to look. Sancerre is white."

Now Arthur has put up with his wine snob friend for many years, tolerating arrogance and insult. Generally if I say a bottle is white, it's white, but at this particular moment the problem is not oenological but visual, and Arthur is staring right at the bottle.

Before I can begin my sermon on the wines of the Loire Valley, Arthur appears at the table with the bottle. He places it in front of me and says, "What color does this appear to be?"

There are two other couples surrounding the table. Everyone has heard the dialogue. The evidence appears: The Sancerre is unmistakably red.

Indeed it is an unusual bottle; a red Sancerre is rarely seen in the United States. It is sold in England, however, and obviously in France. In fact, any red wine from the Loire Valley is uncommon. When one speaks of Loire Valley wines, one speaks of whites—some of the most pleasant and reasonably priced white wines in the world. Still, the wine snob, listening to somebody who is *looking* at the bottle, might contemplate the possibility of a red. Not likely. He is always so convinced of the sanctimony of his erudition—is so convinced that he knows everything and nobody else knows anything—that he is blinded to possibilities. And having declared, in the face of all likelihood to the contrary, that this bottle must be white, he is condemned to a dinner of embarrassment and humiliation.

Death of the Wine Snob—end of Act II.

This is reasonable advice: A Zinfandel can be white; a Sancerre can be red. A Beaujolais, thought of as a light red wine, can be white. Cabernet Sauvignon, thought of as a strong red wine, can also be white. Château Haut-Brion, one of the world's great red Bordeaux, makes a white, although not in the same class as the red. But if someone shouts up from the cellar that he has a white Haut-Brion, believe him. He is looking at the bottle.

A WINE
BY ANY OTHER
NAME

A bunch of us black-belt wine snobs were sitting around at dinner discussing some of the urgent social matters of the hour, like whether or not the '61 Latour was ready to drink—a conversation, which among wine snobs, could last three days. The waiter arrived, and Reginald, our guiding spirit, ordered a Châteauneuf-du-Pape with mignonettes of lamb bordelaise. We turned to him aghast.

"Surely, Reginald, a red Bordeaux would be more compatible," someone said.

"Possibly a Clos de Vougeot, or any good red Burgundy would be more subtle."

"Perhaps even a Rhine," I said, straining to appear both daring and sophisticated. "Why are you ordering a Châteauneuf-du-Pape?"

"Because I like the way it sounds," said Reginald.

Indeed, it has been said of Châteauneuf-du-Pape that more bottles have been ordered because of the name than because of the wine. It may also be true of Pouilly-Fuissé and Beaujolais; there's something elegant about rolling those delightful sounds off the tongue.

And so, while there is much talk about the character of wine—the nose, the balance, the color—there is an underworld argument that says wine is ordered because of its name. Wine snobs fear to admit it, but privately concede that they prefer the sound of a snappy Pouilly-Fuissé to a cumbersome and plodding Muscadet.

Therefore the time has come to confess this secret failing of connoisseurs and to list the five great wine names (and the five not-so-great).

1. It would be difficult to steal top honors from *Châteauneuf-du-Pape* although there is some dis-

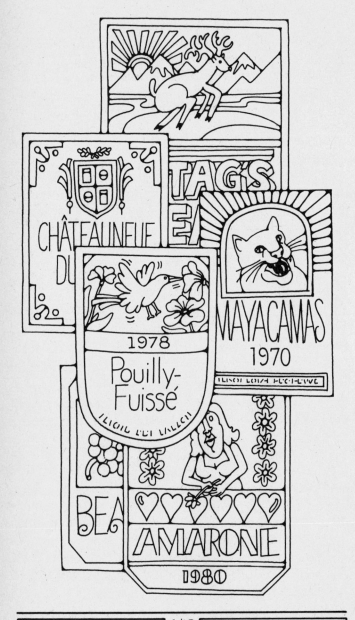

parity between the quality of the name and the quality of the wine. It's not that the wine is bad; it's perfectly sound, hearty Rhone Valley wine, excellent with beef stew or game. But it is no better than ordinary in the wine hierarchy, surpassed by so many red Burgundies, red Bordeaux and Spanish Riojas. But ah, the name. Nothing surpasses the curious poetry and peculiarity of Châteauneuf-du-Pape.

2. *Pouilly-Fuissé* is second—a charming, flutelike sound, like the flight of a hummingbird or a quickly stolen kiss. It is delicacy and melody combined, and the absolutely perfect wine for a young man to order on his first date with a lovely and impressionable woman. And after the impression the wine stands up: a dry and fruity white Burgundy. Indeed, where can you get good wine and a solo on the flute all at the same time?

3. *Mayacamas*—the curious, throaty sound of the viola—is difficult at first to love. It sounds like an Inca emperor, but is in fact an Indian word meaning "howl of the mountain lion." On this alone it is worth ordering because someone at the table is certain to ask what it means.

Mayacamas is one of California's premium wineries, bottling an excellent Chardonnay as well as first-rate Cabernet Sauvignon and Zinfandel. The name has a certain pied beauty which transcends curiosity; it has marvelous resonance, mystery and a haunting melody.

4. *Amarone* is one of the great Italian red wines, a wine of incredible depth, bouquet and breed. Forget about that, however, and listen to the name—preferably pronounced by Luciano Pavarotti—Ammahr-roh-nay; a siren song, a seduction.

There was once a young man, hopelessly in love, and yet the love was not shared. So he took her to a secluded Italian restaurant, in a quiet corner, and ordered Amarone. It was seven pounds—more than he could afford—but his heart was past such considerations. He pronounced it perfectly—Amarone—and the waiter stood at attention, raised his eyebrows, and repeated it. "I think we have only one bottle left," he said. The wine was velvet. And the sound? It was like Heifetz playing Schubert, and their hearts were joined forever.

5. *Stag's Leap*—and here comes an argument. How could I—you are thinking—follow Amarone with Stag's Leap; the strings with percussion? Well, an orchestra is many sounds, and one of the good sounds—one of the great names—is Stag's Leap. Another of the small, premium California wineries, Stag's Leap is prized for its Petite Sirah as well as its Chardonnay. Most important, it has this bizarre, muscular name that conjures up memories of Teddy Roosevelt attacking at San Juan Hill. Perhaps at one time this might have been a trifle too combative to qualify as a great wine name, but we have had enough melody and enough curiosity, and what we need is a bit of Americana to celebrate the emergence of California wines. Don't think you have to study wine snobbery at the Sorbonne. They give a good course in the Napa Valley. Today, snobbery is international.

What a pity that wineries bottling excellent wine have no sense of the drama or the elegance of the name. Perfume companies name their products Chanel or Réplique; wineries are named Schramsberg and Gallo.

Don't expect Reginald to admit it, but here are the five names that dedicated wine snobs ignore.

1. Some of the worst names make the best wines, and *Muscadet* leads the list. The name has no majesty, a perfectly common union of sounds and syllables that really belongs on a can of beer. The wine, however, is lovely, a fruity, semi-dry wine from the Loire Valley. It is almost always the best value on any restaurant's wine list. That's because nobody wants to say Muscadet when they can say Pouilly-Fuissé for only a few pounds more a bottle.

2. *Schloss Vollrads*. It seems unfair to include the German wines on the list of the five worst names, the language being so guttural, but then again a bad name is a bad name. In fairness to the

Germans I am limiting the five-worst list to one classic example. Others might reasonably argue that Germany could run away with all five places.

I don't think I need dwell on why Schloss Vollrads is a terrible name for a wine or almost anything else. There it is, right in front of you, like a locomotive puffing and steaming into the Berlin station.

3. *Gallo*, which produces a Chenin Blanc and Colombard that are constantly knocking off premium wineries in comparative tastings, still is named Gallo. The name belongs—instead of Aunt Millie—on a jar of marinara sauce.

4. *Gewürztraminer.* If you wanted to open a sausage shop—hang giant liverwursts and salamis right in the window—a terrific name for the shop would be Gewürztraminer. It has that husky, Polish/Hungarian melody; that sausage, hot mustard and sauerkraut flavor. Indeed, if the Alsatians (whose wine this is) had not named their national sauerkraut-and-sausage dish choucroute, they might have used Gewürztraminer. It's just right— but it's all wrong for a wine. The wine is a spicy, flowery white from the eastern border of France and it deserved a better name. A pity. Fourth place to Gewürztraminer.

5. Maybe *Barsac* isn't *such* a terrible-sounding name, but the French should have known better. Barsac would be appropriate for a cooking sherry, the bottle wrapped in burlap. The wine is rarely served in restaurants. It is a dessert wine, and unless there is a gathering of six or eight—and unless people are used to dessert wines—it is never ordered. In fact, even in a large group, people would order a Sauternes, which is better known and more melodic.

So there are the five worst—clumsy, plodding, guttural names—that sound simply awful in the company of fine crystal and silver. Which wine snob, I ask you, will order a Schloss Vollrads—a sound likened to a tire going flat—when he could have an Amarone and a thousand violins?

REGINALD

I bumped into Reginald at the library recently where he was studying the precipitation charts in the upper Médoc during 1917. While I cannot personally see this as a matter of consuming interest, it could be everyday conversation in the circle that Reginald frequents.

Afterwards we had coffee and discussed wine. Naturally we discussed wine. Had I inquired about the weather or about some new Broadway show of special interest, I would have been permitted to watch Reginald consume a cup of coffee in under sixty seconds.

Reginald doesn't deny that he is a wine fanatic— nor does he apologize. Those are his rules. They are a bit disconcerting but at least you know where you're at. You want to discuss theatre? You have coffee with someone else.

There are a number of people who regard Reginald's conduct as rude and antisocial. Their point seems to be that Reginald should discuss issues of general concern. They claim this is the way social discourse is conducted—a sharing of interests and ideas. Reginald says that he doesn't care about social discourse; he cares about wine. Furthermore, he says, nobody *else* is interested in social discourse either. Their sole purpose in listening is to mark time until they can get the conversation on their own track. So much for sharing ideas, he says.

I don't think I want to mention whether I agree with Reginald or not, my own level of social activity being at something less than whirlwind pace. But I don't think he is all wrong. Occasionally I suggest that a less rigid attachment to a single subject might improve his image and open new social possibilities, but Reginald says that is pure hypocrisy.

"This is the way I am," he says. "Some people respect me, and this is what they respect me for. Others don't, and that's quite all right. You are suggesting that I present a person that is not me, so that they will. What would be the satisfaction in that? They wouldn't be respecting *me* anyway."

So Reginald goes his independent way, wearing an antique watch chain, buying his suits exclusively from Brooks Brothers, and ordering his shirts by mail. Styles come and styles go; ties get wide and ties get narrow. It means nothing to Reginald. Even language changes: One month everyone is saying, "Have a nice day." The next month everyone is saying, "I could care less." All of that blows past Reginald like an autumn breeze. Fashions change in restaurants and nightclubs: Studio 54s come and go; people stand on line; people beg to get in. Reginald never knew where Studio 54 was. And of course there is fashion in wines and spirits. One year it is Kirs, the next it is Campari. Reginald drinks wine according to traditions that began with Thomas Jefferson.

Stodgy and exasperating, without flair, without ornament, Reginald goes his way and drinks his wine. Some respect him; that's quite nice. Some resent him; that's O.K. Reginald would say that he lives twenty-four hours a day with Reginald. My god, what a philosophy—and this is our leader; this is the high priest of wine snobbery. Are you sure you want to be a wine snob?

REGINALD
RECONSIDERED

There is a special delight in discovering Reginald's idiosyncrasies and indiscretions as there would be a special delight in discovering the indiscretions of any high priest. Indiscretion is always delicious, and the higher the office the more delicious it is. Some may feel this comparison is strained, but among Reginald's followers in the religion of wine snobbery it seems perfectly reasonable.

Since the emerging wine snob must sooner or later encounter Reginald, it might be helpful to mention some of his idiosyncrasies, lest that person commit some grave error of judgment. For instance, one might, as a show of appreciation for some small favor, give Reginald a gift. He might, for example, choose a necktie, and that necktie might—as neckties often do these days—have someone's initials embroidered on it. I *know* he might because I know someone who did, and that someone has been notably absent at all wine events for the past several years.

Reginald gets furious over initials—his own or the designer's. "Why do I need my initials on things?" he argues. "I know what my initials are." His intensity somewhat concerns his friends, who listen to him and think, So don't engrave your initials, Reginald; no one will care one way or the other.

The story is reliably told that Reginald once received a gift certificate from a shop that he does not usually frequent, and needing a solid burgundy tie for one of his several dark-grey suits, he brought the certificate to the necktie department. The salesman reached up to the shelf, withdrew a satiny wine-colored tie, and laid it with a flourish across the glass counter. As Reginald's eye traveled the length of the tie he noticed three initials, intertwined. "What is that?" he asked.

"Y-S-L," said the salesman. "Yves Saint Laurent. Our better ties are all designer-initialed."

"That's very nice," said Reginald, slowly turning the color of the tie, "but let me have one of your cheaper ties without the initials."

There was an edge to Reginald's voice, and the salesman proceeded cautiously. "Ah yes, they do seem to have everything initialed these days, don't they? But I'm afraid that just at this moment we do not have a burgundy necktie without initials." He knotted the tie, perhaps to bring Reginald's attention away from the point, but of course he could not measure the fury of his customer. Someone who was with Reginald swears that he saved the salesman's life by diverting Reginald's attention to a forthcoming tasting of California dessert wines.

Reginald also borders on the insane in the matter of clothing with reptile appliqués. "It's a nice shirt," he says, "but what does the alligator do for it?"

I have it on authority that Reginald once wrote the alligator company and told them how much he liked their shirt. He also told them that he wasn't fond of the emblem and that he would like to place a special order for three shirts without the alligator: one tan, one navy, one red.

The alligator company wrote back that they appreciated his interest and his kind comments but they had never considered manufacturing the shirt without the emblem (this being contrary to their merchandising image) and even if they would do it, the minimum order would be 3,500 shirts.

Reginald replied that he could increase his order to six shirts if they would add a yellow, a magenta,

and a forest green, but that was as far as he could go. The company did not respond, an oversight that Reginald regarded as insolent, and he has carried this affront with him for many years. Happily, alligator emblems do not generally decorate the attire worn at wine tastings, although they appear to be working their way in that direction.

Other topics wisely avoided in Reginald's company are surprise birthday parties, parades, rooftop restaurants, class reunions, the collected works of Kahlil Gibran, notes that begin "From the desk of . . ." and the paintings of Leroy Neiman. I told you that Reginald has a lot of idiosyncrasies.

I hate to dwell on Reginald, but this is or pretends to be a guide to wine snobbery. The emerging wine snob will one day appear at an event of The Wine and Food Society or La Chaîne des Rôtisseurs neatly attired in his snappy new Countess Mara tie. There he will meet Reginald and there he will be judged—as though by Saint Peter at the Pearly Gates.

Do you want to get into heaven or not?

IN DEFENSE
OF WINE
SNOBBERY

Whatever Reginald's idiosyncrasies he is a formidable opponent in any discussion on wine snobbery. Over the years he has listened, not always patiently, to the banter and ridicule that necessarily accompany the style and protocol of wine drinking. He has listened to his friends reasonably discuss with the sommelier the comparative merits of the 1970 and 1971 Château Simard to the embarrassment and chagrin of everyone sitting at the table. He has observed the traded glances of shared boredom when a wine discussion occurs at a dinner party. He has heard the abuse heaped upon any wine enthusiast sufficiently naïve to anticipate that anyone would want to hear about a vertical tasting of Château Pétrus. And over the years, little by little, Reginald has gotten steamed up.

Deciding perhaps that it is his mission to defend the wine snob—if he won't, who will?—Reginald argues fiercely that wine snobbery is the same as any other kind of snobbery. I think I agree with him.

Consider that, at any restaurant in America, two couples are having Martinis. One Tanqueray, one Beefeater, one Gordon's, one Smirnoff. One dry, one not-so-dry, two absolutely dry or else. One olive, one onion, one twist, one nothing. Three straight up, one on the rocks. It requires a computer specialist from IBM to keep these records straight. Are these Martini snobs?

Are Martini snobs worse than wine snobs?

We are talking with friends and the conversation turns to tennis. Never mind that everyone doesn't *play* tennis, there will soon follow a dissertation on the comparative advantages of wood and graphite racquets. That should not exceed a half hour, even including some gentle but unmistakable references to the new two-hundred-pound graphite models. Next comes tennis shoes: Do you wear Puma or Adidas? Following that comes court surfaces: Do you prefer to play on clay or grass?

"Oh, you've never played on grass? What a pity. Perhaps if you ever get a chance to play in Europe . . ."

That conversation only lasts fifteen minutes because everyone is saving himself for the major discussion: tennis elbows. Any group of tennis players can keep going on elbows for the entire evening.

"Dr. Cooper, at Park and Fifty-seventh, has me doing isometrics. Who are you seeing? Dr. Mancuso? I'm not sure I've heard of him."

Are these tennis snobs? Are tennis snobs worse than wine snobs?

Although it is generally accepted thinking that no snob is as bad as the wine snob, I believe that all snobs are about equal. The wine snob, however, suffers from a particular phenomenon: *the language of wine*. Châteauneuf-du-Pape is a strange word, as is Pouilly-Fuissé. They don't sound like Pabst Blue Ribbon or Miller High Life. Regular guys don't go around saying "Pouilly-Fuissé."

And what about all that stuff about "years"? Tanqueray doesn't have good years and bad years. Jack Daniel's is Jack Daniel's in 1971 and 1973. But Burgundy is not the same: 1971 was a distinctly better year for Burgundy than was 1973. Is the wine lover expected to order Burgundy in a year that was not as good?

And how about twirling and sniffing? If you do any twirling at McSorley's Ale House on East Seventh Street you could seriously endanger your health. But the wine drinker twirls his wine around the glass. How to explain that? Well, actually, fairly easily; twirling a wine, especially a red, releases the bouquet and exposes the wine to air, softening it. It is the sensible thing to do when you are drinking wine but there is no escaping the suggestion of pretense. We don't twirl Martinis.

So the wine drinker is trapped by the choreography of wine. Every question he asks, every movement he makes, has the appearance of affectation. And the *natural* manner of an intelligent and interested wine drinker appears to be mere pomp and ceremony.

What can he do? Nothing. You can't change the language of wine and you can't change the customs and traditions.

There is simply no way to say to the wine waiter, "Let it breathe a few minutes; it's not quite ready," without embarrassing everyone at the table.

So the wine snob is trapped. Even if he is modest—even if he is unassuming—the language he uses, the years he has remembered, the sniffing and the twirling gang up on him. He needn't gesture grandly; he needn't pontificate. He wears the cloak of wine snobbery.

His defense? There is no defense, although I have often heard Reginald refer to the words of Henry Ford II: "Never complain. Never explain."

My god, Reginald, couldn't you have found something out of Shakespeare?

The character of Reginald—arrogant, imperious, intolerant, impatient—may bear a certain resemblance to various wine enthusiasts around town. If anyone is troubled by the question "Is Reginald me?" the answer is—

Yes.